To Sheila Bryant

Thanks You & God Bless

Rev. H. Wallace

10/17/96

Federal Plantation

Affirmative <u>Inaction</u>
Within Our
Federal Government

Howard L. Wallace

Duncan & Duncan, Inc.,
<u>*Publishers*</u>

We gratefully acknowledge permission to re-print brief quotes from: *The Federal Employees' News Digest* (several editions); *Reflections of an Affirmative Action Baby* by Stephen L. Carter © 1991, Harper Collins; *A Conflict of Rights—The Supreme Court and Affirmative Action* by Melvin Urofsky © 1991, Simon & Schuster; *The Rage of a Privileged Class by* Ellis Cose © 1993, Harper Collins; *Sue Your Boss and Remedies for Employment Discrimination* by E. Richard Larson © 1981, Farrar, Straus, Giroux; "How to Make Diversity Pay" by Faye Rice © *Fortune,* 1994 Time, Inc.; "Mikulski Introduces Fair Employment Legislation for Capitol's 2300 Workers" and "In Maryland Delegation Only Bentley Has No Black or Hispanic Aides" by Michael A. Fletcher © 1994, *The Baltimore Sun;* "IQ, Is It Destiny?" by Tom Morganthau © 1994, *Newsweek.*

Published by *Duncan & Duncan, Inc., Publishers*
Mailing address: P.O. Box 1137, Edgewood, MD 21040
Phone: 410-538-5579: Fax: 410-538-5584

Library of Congress Catalog Card Number: 95-83171

Wallace, Howard L., –
Federal Plantation: Affirmative Inaction Within Our Federal Government
1. Affirmative Action 2. Afro-Americans, in Federal Government
3. Employment Discrimination 4. Federal Government, Discrimination 5. Federal Government, Employment

ISBN 1-878647-24-5

Biblical passages shown in this book are from the King James version of the Bible, except where otherwise noted.

9-8-7-6-5-4-3-2-1

Dedication

To my mother, Mrs. Agnes M. Little, and the memory of James C. Little, her eldest son who died of the AIDS virus in September 1995.

Acknowledgments

I give honor and praise to my Lord and Savior, Jesus Christ, who allowed me to write this book; to my wife, Tanya (who I affectionately call TJ), and to my children, Courtney, Brandon, and Lauren. I thank all of you for your patience. You are my strength and together our strength comes from God.

Preface

My mother served the Federal government faithfully for 34 years, but because of her race and gender she was never able to rise above the grade of GS-5. She knew all too well the cruel injustices thousands of federal minority employees faced every day.

On her meager earnings she raised 5 children and kept the nucleus of the family intact. She was a widow having lost her husband in an ill-fated airplane crash while he was serving his country as a member of the armed forces.

My brother worked for the Department of Social Services in Maryland and though he was not a federal employee, the racial injustices are no less at the state level. In his dying days we talked extensively about America's version of apartheid within our government system.

Their stories echo the voices of African-Americans

everywhere who serve this country faithfully everyday. They work just as hard as their white counterparts and on average are paid less, disciplined more often, hired last and fired first. God has always known this story and like the scribes of old, He has commanded me to write it. This book is the product of a Mother's love and a brother's memory.

Howard L. Wallace

Foreword

M y first meeting with Howard L. Wallace was at a Military Post in Aberdeen, Maryland in the Spring of 1991. He was a guest speaker at my newly adopted church. He carried himself with self confidence and assurance. As a white male who had very little interaction with African-Americans prior to entering the military, his commanding presence intimidated me.

However, once he began to boldly preach, I was captivated by how clearly and persuasively he stated his message on the importance of faith. I was later to realize that God had given me a special kinship with this man who is full of love, compassion, and has a burning desire to do God's will.

It was ironic how God led me, a shy white male raised in the suburbs of the state of Florida, to mentor under an outgoing black male raised in the inner city of

Baltimore, Maryland. Our common denominator before Jesus Christ was the fact that we both were raised in a matriarchal home. Neither of us had much interaction with our fathers. I believe God has used this similarity to strengthen our bond of fellowship.

As our relationship developed, I have grown to admire him as a father, a trusting friend, and a fellow ambassador for Jesus Christ. Like most Americans, I am deeply troubled by the moral depravity of our country. That is why I am thankful this book was written. Each chapter presents clear factual examples about the perpetuation of racial discrimination within our government.

Howard is not afraid to go head-on with complex issues of public policy. His experience serving in the military and working as a civilian for the Federal government has given him an inside look at how our current day system compares to the standards set by our forefathers, who designed this great country to ensure equality for all people. He gives a solid understanding of major issues surrounding racism within the government. He also provides valuable examples about how we can restore our American heritage based on biblical values.

In this book, Howard not only supplies information to capture your attention, but also causes you to examine your own beliefs. The book is refreshingly candid and equips you with enough wisdom to become proactive in the fight for a better America. *Federal*

Plantation: Affirmative Inaction Within Our Federal Government is a must read for all Americans during these times of racial strife and division.

The relentless assault against affirmative action must cease, so that the healing process can began. When history records the fruit of this labor, it may well be said that this book became the social conscience of this nation at a time when it was truly a house divided.

> *Scott C. Stevens*
> Youth Pastor
> The Christian Service Center

Contents

Introduction   12

1—   Affirmative Action   15
2—   The Myth of Reverse Discrimination   21
3—   The Reagan AMBush on the
     Supreme Court   27
4—   Benjamin Can Be **NO BENEFIT** Banneker   32
5—   A Stroll Through the Big House   37
6—   Armed and Able to Discriminate   40
7—   Shh...Discrimination Is a Secret
     at the NSA   52
8—   The Federal Bureau of Investigation—and
     Discrimination   57
9—   The Borders of Racial Justice Are Closed at
     Immigration   62
10— A Disease Out of Control   65
11— Agriculture: The Last Plantation   69
12— Discrimination Is Big Business
     at Commerce   75

Contents

13—   If You Want to Win at the EEOC,
      Produce Photographs of a Lynching   79
14—   The Bell Curve and Those Who Believe
      in It   85
15—   A Blue Print for Change   96
16—   A Survival Guide for African-Americans
      in the Post Democratic Era   111
17—   What to Do When Faced with
      On-the-Job Discrimination   130

Epilogue: Where Do We Go From Here?   137
Selected Bibliography   140
Index   142

Introduction

W e are living in a time I call the Post Democratic Era. The rush towards conservatism, as defined by Newt Gingrich and the freshmen republicans in Congress along with organizations like the Christian Coalition, has begun in earnest. As a fellow Republican, I agree with many of the principles our party espouses such as balanced budgets, school prayer, lower taxes, and a strong national defense. However, I stand in total opposition to their Republicans all-out assault on affirmative action.

Many people are unaware that affirmative action is a republican program started under the Nixon administration. A fellow black republican, Arthur Fletcher, was the brain thrust behind its conception and he is actively petitioning Congress to keep it intact. It is indeed refreshing to see black republicans like Colin Powell and Arthur Fletcher speak out in support of this program which has opened the door for so many qualified blacks and other minorities.

Anti-affirmative action groups, including many of them within the Republican Party are perpetuating a myth of wide spread reverse discrimination against white males. They would have you believe that blacks and other minorities are being selected for positions regardless of their qualifications. This has the effect of labeling affirmative action plans as quotas. This is emphatically not true! Quotas are illegal. Affirmative action attempts to ensure qualified minority applicants are being given equal consideration, and the intent was to develop an awareness among managers that they need to diversify their workforce.

One of the biggest violators of affirmative action is the Federal Government. Within this sector, this book will show conclusively that blacks and other minorities are routinely discriminated against. Managers within the Federal government who are champions of the status quo and other critics of this book will quickly echo the party line which says, "We wholeheartedly support affirmative action, diversification, and equal employment opportunity for all our workers." They will then proudly display the face of the President and the local chain of command along side some verbiage identifying them as an equal opportunity employer.

The problem is all the agencies in this book cannot back their words with deeds. I purposely focus on documented cases of disparate treatment throughout numerous organizations within our government. My goal was to present irrefutable evidence for the opponents of affirmative action and challenge them to do the same with known cases of reverse discrimination.

Federal Plantation tells the story of what minorities, particularly blacks, experience everyday in the workplace. Even though many of us serve this country with pride and distinction, we know all too well that the fruits of our labor are curtailed just because of the color of our skin.

We are thankful to God for where He has brought us, but we will never settle for the mass injustices inflicted upon so many hard working tax paying citizens, who have sworn to uphold the constitution of this great country. May this book not only show forth these injustices but start all of us on a road that will one day lead to a workplace where everyone is treated fairly. The abolishment of affirmative action is not that road.

Howard L. Wallace

CHAPTER 1

Affirmative Action

The legislation and enactment of affirmative action policy has proven to be one of the most controversial issues confronted in the history of the United States government. Why do so many Americans not only disagree with this law, but believe its intent is to employ unqualified minority workers? The answer lies in the unscrupulous use of the media by politicians who gather votes by use of scare tactics in an attempt to divert focus from the historic practice of preferential treatment of white males and the preservation of their status as a privileged class.

The *Academic American Encyclopedia* defines affirmative action as, "A formal effort to provide increased opportunities for women and ethnic minorities, to overcome past patterns of discrimination." The last part of this definition is the key.

The government recognized that past patterns of

discrimination in both the public and private sector effectively limited opportunities and blatantly excluded the upward mobility of women and ethnic minorities, particularly blacks. Accordingly, it was found necessary to enact laws to establish and enforce a rule of inclusion and fairness for those classes of people historically denied equal consideration of opportunities guaranteed by the 14th Amendment of the U.S. Constitution.

Even with the implementation of affirmative action, there is still a "glass ceiling" practice, a technique of manipulating the governments established policy, which keeps minorities from the upper echelons of management and preserves white male dominance and control.

Having looked at a formal definition of affirmative action lets consider my layman's definition that provides further clarification. When an employer is going to hire for a position and a qualified applicant from the under-represented class applies, the employer needs to hire that applicant or show cause why they should not. It is necessary here to point out that opponents of affirmative action often counter with the charge of racial quotas. A quota implies that people are hired, awarded scholarships or government contracts, strictly because of their race or gender even if they are not qualified. This negative perception and cunningly derived interpretation is due to gross misrepresentation of affirmative action intent by its opponents.

Racial quotas are illegal and they have nothing to do with affirmative action. If you go back to my definition, you will see the words qualified applicant. A person who is not qualified for a particular job is not entitled to that job under affirmative action. Furthermore, on the issue of quotas, if an employer has a workforce that is comprised of 94 percent of a particular class of people and 6 percent of another class, which one is the quota? The opponents of affirmative action would have you believe that the 6 percent is a quota. This infers that the 94 percent were hired on merit. Having worked for the Federal government and witnessed nepotism and cronyism first hand, I can say emphatically that a vast proportion of the 94 percent were not hired on merit alone.

Another key point that needs clarification is that all races of people are covered under affirmative action. As an Equal Employment Opportunity Counselor, I would also counsel white males, who did not realize that they were a protected class as well.

In support of affirmative action, Melvin I. Urofsky, author of the book, *A Conflict of Rights, The Supreme Court and Affirmative Action*, argues why such policy is necessary. He states:

"All arguments in favor of affirmative action boil down to the fact that women, blacks, and other minorities have historically suffered discrimination and have been precluded from various educational and economic opportunities. In order for society to eliminate the lasting vestiges of that discrimination, and to realize the potential contributions of all its citizens, it has to take certain steps to allow these groups access to good schools and good jobs. Whether one talks of goals or quotas, the aim is the same: admit more members of the excluded groups into schools; hire them into jobs and job training programs. If, in the past, the majority used a person's race or gender or national origin against him or her in a discriminatory manner, it is now fair to take those same considerations into account, and use them to the person's benefit."

Again, I reiterate that no minority is entitled to a job strictly because of their race or gender. However, Mr. Urofsky adequately portrays the sentiment that the same attributes which were used to perpetuate discrimination should be used to garner a benefit for those who were previously discriminated against.

It is an undeniable fact that white males prospered and flourished under a system that denied women, blacks and other minorities, equal education and economic opportunities. Affirmative action is a way to reverse this destructive course and insure inclusion and equal opportunity for all Americans.

A unique and curious voice of opposition to affirmative action, Stephen L. Carter, author of the book, *Reflections Of An Affirmative Action Baby*, states, "I got into law school because I am black," yet he believes affirmative action is wrong. He feels it," . . . reinforces racist stereotypes by promoting the idea that the black professional cannot aspire to anything more than being the best black." Mr. Carter further believes that affirmative action must be relegated to only providing educational opportunities. His basic premise is that everyone should be held by the same standard when it comes to the job market.

Clearly, Mr. Carter lacks a fundamental knowledge or is oblivious of historically perpetuated discriminatory practices in other areas of American society, which have not yet disappeared. In the absence of discrimination, I would wholeheartedly agree with him. However, the majority has an undeniable track record of erecting artificial and covert barriers that deny well qualified minorities good jobs and equal pay.

As an Equal Opportunity Counselor for the Federal government, I routinely see blatant discrimination against blacks and other minorities. Some white employees who were in middle and upper management were below average performers, yet they repeatedly received exceptional appraisals and monetary performance awards. I am not suggesting that all whites were incompetent and unfair.

However, my eyewitness observation of discriminatory actions within the Federal government is why I so vehemently disagree with Mr. Carter's contention of being held to the same standard. His assertion that affirmative action does more harm to minorities then good is in my view completely erroneous. It is not affirmative action that harms minorities; it is the illusory picture being painted by its opponents in the mind of the public that is doing the damage.

The government recognized that billions of dollars in lost wages and an incalculable amount of self-esteem and dignity were lost by women, blacks, and other minorities to a discriminatory system. Affirmative action allows doors to be opened that have previously remained closed. Although some people would try to dispute affirmative action, the fact remains that the original conditions and reasons why the government enacted such policies still exist, and is therefore, still needed.

The ultimate example of fairness and accountability can be found in the Bible in Proverbs 6:30-31. It says, "Men do not despise a thief, if he steals to satisfy his soul when he is hungry. But if he be found, he shall restore sevenfold; he shall give all the substance of his house." Using Proverbs 6:30-31 as an example, affirmative action is a paltry price to pay for retribution to the discriminated classes.

CHAPTER 2

The Myth of Reverse Discrimination

At the forefront of the affirmative action contro-
versy is the myth of reverse-discrimination. Allegations made by affirmative action opponents suggest that unqualified women, blacks, and minorities
are being hired or awarded higher education and business opportunities at the expense of white males. And
further, if they believe a white male is being discriminated against they become zealots for fairness. They
begin to quote what minorities have been saying all
along, that everyone should go on their own merit.

At face value I would agree with that assertion.
The problem is racially biased application. The truth of
the matter and statistics show conclusively that discrimination, not reverse-discrimination, is rampant
throughout the Federal government.

In the most recent baseball dispute between owners and players, the owners claimed they were losing

money and demanded a salary cap to restore financial stability. The players asked to see their books. The owners refused. This gave the perception that the owners were hiding something and in the mind of the public they lost credibility. In comparison, as a proponent of affirmative action, I say to its opponents, let's open the books! Bring forth your case load of reverse-discrimination charges and stack them against the discrimination perpetuated everyday throughout the Federal government. The comparison would be ludicrous.

While many may feel that discrimination is a phenomenon of the past and believe affirmation action policies are no longer necessary, the fact remains that there is mass under-representation of women and racial minorities in management and decision making positions in the Federal government and the private sector.

The court case which elevated reverse-discrimination to national prominence was the *University of California v. Bakke*. The case arose when Alan Bakke, a white male, was twice rejected for admission to the University of California medical school. The school had instituted a policy of setting aside 16 of 100 positions for racial minorities and Bakke charged that his civil rights were violated under the Equal Protection Clause of the 14th Amendment.

The Supreme Court in a 5-4 decision ruled in favor of Bakke. The Court essentially said that the university had violated the Civil Rights Act of 1964, which prohibits federally funded institutions from excluding any person because of race and contended that Bakke had been discriminated against. Yet, in the same ruling, the Supreme Court held that universities may consider race as a factor in their evaluation criteria for admission and that using race is not inherently discriminatory as long as there is no fixed racial quota. However, as the records of history clearly show, the sheer volume of blatant discrimination against racial minorities dwarfs the occasional Bakke scenario.

White males are particularly leery of affirmative action and go to great lengths to advance the notion of reverse-discrimination. In an article entitled, "DOD Pushing Diversity Hard in Promotions," published in the *Federal Employees News Digest*,[1] September 19, 1994, it was stated that:

"The Defense Department is aggressively pushing for greater recruitment and promotion of minorities, women and persons with disabilities . . . number one personnel policy official, Edwin Dorn, in an August 10 memorandum, has ordered his subordinate managers, who oversee about 300 employees, to consider persons other than white males in all appointments to GS-15 and higher . . . it's likely to create plenty of uncertainty on the part of nondisabled white males trying to move into upper echelon slots."

[1]*Federal Employees News Digest* (published by Federal Employees News Digest, Inc., located in Reston, VA) is a highly regarded weekly newsletter covering all matters related to federal employment.

This was one of the more blunter affirmative action policy statements ever issued by a high ranking official in the Department of Defense (DOD). The directive was so terse that a white male in my office was compelled to write at the bottom of the article, "A white male will not enhance an organization? Should the government concentrate on the best qualified or the one to enhance an organization?" He signed it, John, a white male.

In John's view, DOD was guilty of reverse-discrimination. The fact that employees GS-15 and higher were predominantly white males was irrelevant to him and he totally overlooked the fact that some of these white males were not hired on merit. As far as he was concerned, DOD was going to hire women and other minorities that were less qualified and thus create an inferior pool of managers.

If the system was fair, more women, blacks, and minorities would be employed in the tens of thousands of GS-15 positions and higher. The directive issued by DOD was born out of frustration with a system that effectively employs a glass ceiling which inhibits the upward mobility of women and racial minorities, particularly blacks.

The Federal government recognized that a glass ceiling existed within both the public and private sector and addressed the issue in Title II of the Civil Rights Act of 1991. Section 202 of the Act states that, "Congress finds that despite a dramatically growing presence in the workplace, women and minorities remain under-represented in management and decision making positions in business . . ."

The very fact that the government acknowledges a glass ceiling suggest it does not believe women or racial minorities are under-represented because they are not qualified, but is directly related to continued discriminatory practices. Regardless of the statistics and facts which overwhelmingly support the need for affirmative action, its opponents continue to attack and vehemently oppose policies that are intended to promote opportunities and fairness for the historically discriminated classes.

In the book, *The Rage Of A Privileged Class*, its author, Elliot Cose, writes about a conversation he had with a white male Harvard student on the issue of affirmative action. He says the student was very upset about a Supreme Court ruling on the affirmative action question, and began a diatribe about "unqualified minorities demanding preferential treatment at the expense of hard working whites." Cose writes:

"When the young man paused to catch his breath, I took the occasion to observe that it seemed more than a bit hypocritical of him to rage on about preferential treatment. A person of modest intellect, he had gotten into Harvard largely on the basis of family connections.

"His first summer internship, with the White House, had been arranged by a family member. His second, with the World Bank, had been similarly arranged. Thanks to his nice internships and Harvard degree, he had been promised a coveted slot in a major company's executive training program. In short, he was already well on his way to a distinguished career—a career made possible by preferential treatment."

Mr. Cose goes on to say that his words did not have any effect on the young man. This type of reaction is typical of the opponents of affirmative action. They desire to continue reaping benefits from a system which routinely discriminates against women, blacks and other minorities, and to go on parlaying the "good old boy network" into promotions and awards, while simultaneously lambasting affirmative action and crying reverse-discrimination.

Is it realistic to believe that we can go from a society which openly discriminated against women and other minorities for hundreds of years to one that judges totally on merit? This is the epitome of hypocrisy and a blot upon our national conscience.

Reverse-discrimination is a counter charge to affirmative action. Its intent is to undermine its credibility and effectiveness in bringing about equal opportunity for qualified women, blacks, and minorities. Contrary to popular belief, affirmative action is not a hand out, but is an admission that the continued practice of status quo is inherently discriminatory. Let's now take a look at what the Reagan and Bush years did to affirmative action.

CHAPTER 3

The Reagan AMBush
on the Supreme Court

As a conservative I voted for Reagan and Bush. As strongly as I supported their agenda, I am equally opposed to their actions in regards to civil rights. The twelve year reign of the Reagan/Bush administrations set in motion the beginning of decline and reversal of established affirmative action policies. The most damage was done in the appointment of anti-affirmative action Justices to the Supreme Court.

The initial impact of the Reagan/Bush administration appointments to the highest court became evident in the case of the *City of Richmond v. J.A. Croson Company*, where Croson, a white owned company, challenged a minority business utilization "set-aside" plan adopted by the City of Richmond after it found that only 1 percent of African-American businesses were getting city contracts, despite the fact that they made up 50 percent of the population. The city further recognized that this was directly related to the general conduct of the construction industry in the area, in the state, and around the nation in which discrimination and exclusion on the basis of race were widespread.

The plan required non-minority-owned contractors awarded city construction contracts, to subcontract at least 30 percent of the dollar amount of the contract to one or more minority business enterprises. Croson claimed that the plan was unconstitutional under the Equal Protection Clause of the Federal Constitution's Fourteenth Amendment.

In spite of the reasoning by the City of Richmond in establishing the set-aside ordinance, and the obvious imbalance created by the discriminatory practices by the construction industry nationally, the Court ultimately ruled 6 to 3 against the city's plan. The Court said that:

". . . the city had not established a compelling reason for the plan, and had not tied the 30 percent figure to the actual degree of discrimination attributable to the city, and that where none of the evidence presented by the city pointed to any identified discrimination in the city's construction industry, and because past societal discrimination alone could not serve as the basis for such a rigid racial preference."

The late Supreme Court Justice Thurgood Marshall, one of the three justices who voted in dissent, summed up the reality of the decision in his dissenting opinion.

He writes: "The Court's decision marked a step backward in the court's affirmative action jurisprudence. . . the case at hand was readily resolved, so long as one viewed the city's local evidence of discrimination against the backdrop of systematic nationwide racial discrimination which Congress, in enacting the set-aside program, had identified in the construction industry. . ."

The Supreme Court decision in Croson delivered a tremendous blow to the authority of state and city governments in establishing set-aside ordinances where it is apparent that customary discriminatory practices continue to thrive. Aren't they suppose to be the greatest legal minds in America? What if the statistics were reversed and only 1 percent of the City of Richmond contracts were going to white construction businesses? Would the majority of the court have ruled against the ordinance? These are disturbing questions, yet the answers are disturbingly clear.

In the same year of the Croson decision the Court also made it easier for employers to justify a racial imbalance in their workforce. Before the Reagan dominated Court came on the scene, an employers racial imbalance could infer discrimination. In his book, *How to Sue Your Boss*, E. Richard Larson writes:

"As the Supreme Court has stated, 'Imbalance is often a telltale sign of . . . discrimination; absent explanation, it is ordinarily to be expected that nondiscriminatory . . . practices will in time result in more or less representative of the racial and ethnic [religious and sexual] composition of the population in the community. . .'"

Although the pre-Reagan AMBush court had ruled that burden of proof was on the employer to prove that a racial imbalance was not discriminatory, this position was weakened in the landmark case *Wards Cove Packing v. Atonio*. The Court ruled 5 to 4 that the plaintiff must prove discrimination by identifying the specific practice which caused it. The Court essentially said, "The ultimate burden of proving that discrimination against a protected group has been caused by a specific employment practice remains with the plaintiff at all times."

The notion that employers no longer have to justify racial imbalances is absolutely frightening. When one looks at the dismal record of an employers willingness to hire qualified minorities, these rulings only compound the problem and is further indicative of the Republican position on the issue of affirmative action. They somehow derive and believe, in spite of evident practices of discrimination, that employers will hire the most qualified applicants regardless of race or gender.

Clearly, the decisions in *Croson* and *Atonio* were severe setbacks for affirmative action. These decisions reverberated throughout halls of legislative bodies across the country, and created the precedent to roll back affirmative action gains.

Both the Reagan and Bush administrations advanced policies which would protect the status quo and freeze in place a discriminatory system which promotes and maintains the racial imbalances that exist throughout our society. By taking away employer accountability, limiting higher education opportunities, and thwarting programs which provide for minority business growth, this administration tacitly endorsed discrimination.

Reagan and Bush fought the idea of protectionism when it involved free trade, but on the issue of affirmative action they are in fact protectionist. By taking away employer accountability for erecting artificial barriers that hinder the hiring and upward mobility of minorities, this administration gave employees a green light to discriminate.

In the next chapter, we will look at a case that epitomizes the influence Reagan and Bush had over the Justice decisions regarding affirmative action.

CHAPTER 4

Benjamin Can Be
NO BENEFIT Banneker

The impact of the judicial appointments to the federal bench during the Reagan/Bush administration was also felt in relation to higher education. In the case of *Daniel J. Podberesky v. University of Maryland*, Podberesky, an Hispanic student, sued the University of Maryland because he was rejected as a scholarship applicant for a blacks-only scholarship program, the Benjamin Banneker Scholarship, that provided full tuition, as well as room and board to approximately 80 black students a year.

In an October 28, 1994, article titled "Judges Forbid Scholarships Based On Race," written by Marcia Myers, a *Baltimore Sun* staff writer, Podberesky contended that the program gave preferential treatment to blacks at the expense of other students. The University of Maryland fully supported the program and believed it to be totally justified in offering the scholarship. But yet, the three-judge panel residing over the case was quoted as saying, "We are no longer talking about the kind of discrimination for which a race-conscience remedy may be prescribed."

The American Council on Education president, Robert H. Atwell, rallied behind the college and encouraged other universities to in his words, ". . . keep open the door of opportunity to American higher education." Further, George Keller, retired chairman of the department of higher education at the University of Pennsylvania stated:

"The purpose of the scholarships was to redress a particular injustice, so for others to say they were unfairly excluded misses the point. The addressing of the wrongs of the past really has to go to the one group we systematically excluded. It wasn't too long ago that Thurgood Marshall wasn't allowed into the University of Maryland law school."

Scholarship programs initiated by college universities provide educational opportunities for those classes of people who were in the past denied admission and the opportunity for higher education. It is also an acknowledgment of their responsibility in reversing the ugly trend of racial exclusion.

Judicial decisions which oppose institutions that attempt to diversify and open windows of opportunity for minorities are a direct result of the Reagan/ Bush appointees to the federal bench. In a November 1994 edition of *USA Today,* the gender and racial makeup of the judges appointed to the federal bench by the last three presidents was reported.

During the Reagan administration, 97 percent of the judges appointed were white; 5 percent were female; 1 percent were black; and 1 percent were Hispanic. Bush was only slightly more sympathetic towards minorities. During his term 95 percent of his appointees were white; 10 percent were female; 2.5 percent were black; and 2.5 percent were Hispanic. Of the 95 percent that were white, 90 percent were male.

Republicans would have us believe that the Reagan and Bush white male appointees to the federal bench were the most qualified judges available. The truth is, these appointees were chosen because they embodied the beliefs of the appointing president and not necessarily because they were the best qualified. Isn't this a quota?

What's the difference between a white male quota and a quota promoting diversity? In fact, the judges appointed during the Reagan/Bush years were probably chosen to safeguard the privilege and power of the white male against the inroads of a perceived minority threat to their status.

On the other hand, President Clinton has so far appointed a racial mix of judges to the federal bench that more closely mirror the racial makeup of American society. Of his appointees, 69 percent were white; 31 percent were female; 22 percent were black; and 8 percent were Hispanic. Of the 69 percent that were white, about the same percentage were males.

The same Republicans who would support the Reagan/Bush racial mix of judicial appointees would say that President Clinton has resorted to quotas at the expense of white males. It does not matter that the majority of Clinton's appointees were white males. In their view too many are female, black, or Hispanic. This racial mix alone constitutes a quota in their narrow perspective of affirmative action.

If the issue is that quotas are illegal, how do judges determine what qualifies as a quota? In the absence of affirmative action, are not minorities at a huge disadvantage? Obviously, any effort to diversify could be held hostage to the same legal barriers which confronted the Benjamin Banneker Scholarship program at the University of Maryland.

We have come to a time where judges appointed by the Reagan/Bush administrations are deciding that race discrimination is no longer a problem in America. Based on this dangerous and erroneous assumption, they are making legal decisions which are negatively impacting affirmative action and ultimately an intrusion upon the civil rights of millions of American citizens.

Earlier I challenged the opponents of affirmative action to bring forth empirical evidence that this law has caused widespread reverse discrimination against white males. It certainly would not be wise to challenge my opponents without providing evidence of my own to support the need for a strong affirmative action law.

In the next few chapters, we'll take a look at the track record of the different federal agencies and the various branches of service in regards to their employment practices.

CHAPTER 5

A Stroll Through the Big House

W hen one begins to seriously review the governments commitment to civil rights and affirmative action, its only appropriate to start at the hallowed halls of Congress from which the nation's laws and policies originate.

In an article entitled, "Mikulski Introduces Fair Employment Legislation for the Capitol's 2,300 Workers," published in the *Baltimore Sun*, by Michael A. Fletcher, it was reported that a General Accounting Office (GAO) study found that a "hostile and racially discriminatory work environment" was the norm for the Capitol's workers who maintain the 285 acre complex.

Most significant, the GAO report revealed the agency not only lacked a basic employee management system, but that blacks languished in low-level jobs. In addition, the GAO study uncovered the following:

- Minorities and women are under-represented in the agency's better paying jobs;
- The agency has no formal performance evaluation system; and
- There is no agency-wide merit-based hiring and promotion plan.

The findings of GAO comes as no surprise considering that this is a consistent mode of operation throughout the Federal government. The very fact that these practices exist within the nation's capitol highlights the insensitivity of the Federal government in adhering to equal employment opportunity policies promoted by its legislative body.

This revelation compelled Maryland Senator Barbara Mikulski to introduce legislation requiring that the agency establish a fair employment system. While it is commendable that Senator Mikulski took the initiative to introduce a bill that addresses the problems found by GAO, sadly it is not enough to sway the tide of reluctance to alter tradition and hold its members accountable in adopting fair employment practices within the halls of Congress.

In an article entitled, "In MD. Delegation, Only Bentley Has No Black Or Hispanic Aides," published in the *Baltimore Sun*, by Michael A. Fletcher, it was conveyed that Ms. Bentley did not have any minorities on her staff. Considering that Ms. Bentley represents a district that is 92 percent white, it is common practice for members of Congress to hire aides that helped them get elected or those who embody their political views.

But what was most insulting and proof positive of the GAO reports credibility in its findings was the statement in the article which read, "The Lutherville Republican (Bentley) pointed out her office receptionist is 25 percent American Indian."

It is absurd that a senior member of Congress would not realize that this type of rational is condescending and a major political faux pas. This is an example of the mentality and reasoning of many of the elected officials who legislate the laws for the country.

Let's now take a look at the Department of Defense and see what life is like for minorities on this part of the plantation.

CHAPTER 6

Armed and Able to Discriminate

M any high ranking military and civilian government officials who bear the responsibility of upholding and enforcing the law in regards to the Equal Employment Opportunity (EEO) Program all to often neglect their duties, or regard with total disdain, the existence of these laws. They will elicit support by showing up at events commemorating African-American, Hispanic, or Asian-American history; however, when it comes to substantive support and action, they retreat or engage in evasive tactics to hide the truth.

When confronted about their adherence to EEO guidelines, they rush to gather up all the published policies, blow off the accumulated dust, and display them proudly as verifiable proof of their commitment to EEO.

At an Army installation located in a northern suburb of Baltimore City that is seething in racism and permeated by the "good old boy network," minorities are systematically discriminated against. Because of the severity of this problem, the local chapter of Blacks in Government (BIG), an organization of black federal employees, were compelled to send a letter on behalf of black employees and ask the Commanding General to begin an investigation into the allegations of wide spread discrimination on his post.

The letter contained an outline of the alleged discriminatory practices and a request that he commission a "Glass Ceiling Study" which would determine if minorities were being denied access into the upper echelons of the workforce. The General dutifully responded with a letter promising to look into the matter.

His first "inaction" was to give the BIG letter to his Civilian Personnel Office and told them to respond to the allegations cited. It is important to note here that the personnel office was included in the allegations cited by BIG in the initial letter. He also provided a copy to his Equal Employment Officer (EEO) for comments and recommendations.

Accordingly, both the personnel office and the EEO responded with totally opposite findings and recommendations. The personnel office staff denied every allegation and used the downsizing of the Federal government as the scapegoat for minority discontent. But the EEO Officer substantiated the allegations with statistical data and advised the General to approve the

"Glass Ceiling Study." As expected, the General rejected the EEO's report and bought off on the personnel office's version. He even allowed the personnel staff to write a letter on his behalf and signed it as his official response to BIG. Needless to say, to allow the personnel department to write his response and ignore the recommendations of his primary staff officer is suspect in the least.

Predictably, if the Commanding General was now questioned about racial problems on his post, he would immediately produce the personnel department's report and say that his staff looked into the matter but found that the allegations were unsubstantiated. Yet, concealed beneath the rhetoric and paper trail would be the EEO Officer's recommendations, which was contrary to what the General wanted to see, and which he ignored.

This is the type of affirmative inaction which causes the government numerous EEO cases that cost tax payers millions of dollars foolishly invested in vain and feeble attempts to continue the corrosive custom of mistreatment of the government's minority workforce. Unsurprisingly, this kind of race baited mismanagement is common practice at this installation. Listed are other reported cases of reoccurring race biased personnel practices at this location:

• Four highly qualified black employees, three males and one female, are referred for possible hire to fill seven GS-13 slots in the scientific and chemistry discipline. The agency employed no black employees at the GS-13 level in this field, yet, rejects all four applicants and hires six white males and one white female. The four black applicants file a class action complaint alleging racial discrimination.

• A black male who serves as a budget supervisor at the GS-12 level transfers to installation headquarters and is told he must take a downgrade to a GS-11 because he needed to gain experience at that level. Prior to the transfer he had managed a quarter of a billion dollars and supervised ten employees.

In addition, before being a civilian federal employee, he had been a Captain in the military and was a Company Commander. At the same time of his transfer, a white female was hired as a GS-11 budget analyst and within ninety days she was promoted to a GS-12. The supervisor said she was promoted because she had worked there previously.

In fact, she had worked their previously as a secretary and performed duties totally unrelated to being a budget analyst. The black male was ultimately given back his GS-12 grade after eight months on the job, but only after pressure was brought to bear on the supervisor.

• A black female operates as a budget analyst at the GS-11 grade and is responsible for a multimillion dollar environmental program while her peers work at the GS-12 and 13 levels and manage programs that are less complex and involve less money. Despite the obvious inequity, she applies for an intern position in the environmental career field where the position tops out at the GS-12 level.

The supervisor is given the choice of hiring the black female or his white female secretary. He decides that the white female, who has no degree and only secretarial experience, is more qualified and selects her. The black female, who has a college degree and environmental budgetary experience, takes her case to the Commanding General. Ultimately, her position is upgraded, but she is still a full grade behind her counterparts who are managing less dollars.

• A black male is given the task of turning around a moribund program. Within a year the program becomes a money-maker and is recognized by the Department of the Army for meritorious achievement. Within three years the program generated almost 5 million dollars in direct revenue for his agency, and is selected by the Army's Chief of Staff as the best program in DA (Department of the Army).

The black male is given a total of nine hundred dollars, over a three year period, in award money for his efforts, while his white counterparts are routinely given awards for amounts as high as fifteen hundred dollars a year for accomplishments that are far less noteworthy.

In conclusion, given the severity of the problem at this particular installation, it is reasonable to believe that these modes of discriminatory procedures prevail on other military installations as well.

In an August 16, 1993 article published in the *Federal Times*,[2] by Christy Harris entitled, "Black Navy Workers Charge Harassment," black civilian employees in the Department of the Navy outlined similar discriminatory practices. Here are some of the allegations:

- They are stuck in low paying jobs while white workers are promoted.
- Promotion policies are unfair.
- There is a "Buddy System" in regards to promotions.
- The EEO system is ineffective.
- They are harassed and retaliated against if they file an EEO complaint.

In addition to the above complaints, the article contained the following personal testimonials of discrimination:

- An Accounting Officer was harassed after filing a complaint appealing her performance rating. The manager monitored how long she stayed in the bathroom. He precluded her from using a small space heater at her desk although she had been using it for two years prior to the complaint. The heater was therapeutic for her arthritic legs.

[2] *Federal Times* (published by Army Times Publishing Company in Springfield, VA) is produced to keep federal employees abreast of issues in the civilian sector of the Federal government.

• A GS-9 supervisor said she does some of the same or in some cases more difficult work than the GS-11 Budget Analyst, but the Budget Analyst work is described as "research" while hers is deemed "administrative."

The employees were so frustrated, they enlisted the help of the local chapter of the National Association for the Advancement of Colored People (NAACP).

In fairness to the Navy, the article also reported that the Admiral was "bending over backwards to cooperate" but as encouraging as that may sound, all to often the systemic causes are ignored. This results in a reoccurrence of the same type of problems once the dust settles and the coast is clear. The current system gives no incentives for managers to act responsibly and fairly in personnel matters because there is no personal consequences for their perpetual acts of injustice.

In a *Federal Times* article entitled "Minorities Held Back at Base," writer, Chet Bridger reported that the Equal Employment Opportunity Commission (EEOC) found minorities were being held back by a variety of discriminatory practices at Eglin Air Force Base. The feeling of being discriminated against was so pervasive among black employees at Eglin, that one employee, a black GS-11 Illustrator who claims he was denied a promotion for two years and has a lawsuit pending, was quoted as saying, "Although we have proceeded in time chronologically, the mindset here is still the same: We're white, we're superior, and we're going to take all the jobs."

It was further reported that EEO procedures were lax even though Eglin had settled a $2 million class action lawsuit in 1981. Some of the other EEOC findings were:

- Barriers resulted in only 12.5 percent of minority employees reaching GS-13 and above positions.
- More than half of the EEO complaints filed were ultimately withdrawn. The EEOC said the high rate indicated employees claims of intimidation and retaliation may be credible.
- The EEO office was understaffed. The report found Eglin had only two EEO counselors serving more than 4,500 civilian employees. Regulations require one counselor for every 500 employees. The EEO office employees and collateral duty counselors had limited training.
- EEO counselors were instructed to "tone down" racial slurs and biased language reported in the discrimination complaints.
- EEO counselors failed to maintain data on the issues raised in the complaints, which represented a major noncompliance with EEO reporting requirements.

Base commanders responding to one of the allegations cited in the report said they knew of no instances where employees were intimidated from pursuing an EEO complaint. The Eglin spokesperson was quoted as saying "We want all employees to have faith in the system. We believe we have a good system."

The civil rights leaders who were instrumental in bringing the EEOC investigators to Eglin, believe some of the problems are embedded in the personnel system and could be found at other military installations. A leader of the Southern Christian Leadership Council in Fort Walton Beach, Florida said, "The situation here I think is deeply rooted in the civilian personnel structure. We've got people who have worked there forever who think they are God as far as Eglin Air Force Base goes." The article also listed a number of actions initiated by the Commander at Eglin based upon the EEOC findings. Some of these were:

- Hiring a third counselor.
- Making sure all counselors at the base had received basic and advanced EEO training.
- Installed several procedures to raise the number of promotions among women and minorities making them more reflective of the statistics throughout the government.

Yet, again and again, the same allegations continue to surface no matter what branch of service or government agency is involved. In the book of Matthew, chapter 18:16, the scriptures say, "But if he will not hear thee, then take with thee one or two more, that in the mouth of two or three witnesses every word may be established."

In using Matthew 18:16 as a guide, the allegations put forth thus far are proof of the existence of discrimination, and without doubt would be sufficient in the court of God. But although God may only require two or three witnesses, the opponents of affirmative action apparently require much more.

Accordingly, a class action lawsuit involving 2,700 Hispanic employees at Kelly Air Force Base (AFB) in Florida, was recorded as being the largest lawsuit an Hispanic group has ever brought against the Department of Defense. Again a *Federal Times* article by, Chet Bridger reported that the Hispanics at Kelly AFB believed that they were systematically discriminated against for years and alleged that Hispanic men eligible for promotion to GS-12 and above from 1980 to 1991 were unfairly denied advancement.

The Hispanics based their case on two main factors: the statistical imbalance in upper management and the testimony of two base personnel specialist. At the time of the lawsuit, Hispanics made up 61 percent of the work force at Kelly AFB, but only 21 percent of GS-12 through GS-14 positions in 1981, and 31 percent of these positions in 1991. The personnel specialist interviewed for this report indicated that Hispanics are under-represented at upper levels and that blacks are also discriminated against.

It was further revealed that avoidance tactics are used by management to ensure that their favorite candidates are chosen for promotion. One such tactic talked about was a trial performance evaluation that allows a manager to see where their candidate grades out in comparison to others at the same level. If their candidate doesn't rate well at this juncture, managers may rewrite the variables to insure that their candidate meets the grade.

Another popular ploy noted was the use of details. Managers will detail a person to a position so they can gain valuable experience which allows them to rate higher than a Hispanic applicant.

A spokesman for the group, Manuel Munoz, was quoted as saying, "The Hispanic person can get to a certain point and that's it. It doesn't appear to have been accidental. It's done because our names are much different than theirs." Officials at Kelly AFB contend that race is not a factor in its consideration of promotions. The Deputy Director of Personnel asserted that Hispanics were well represented at all levels of the base work force.

Some may wonder why I included this case since the discriminated class did not involve blacks. A vast majority of whites I have come in contact with believe blacks have a vendetta against the system which clouds our judgment and makes us desire something for nothing. The issue is not about whites against blacks, but is essentially about the Federal government and how it permits its managers to discriminate.

It is common belief by opponents of affirmative action that minorities are chronic complainers who are never satisfied. Contrary to this widely held view, black males, black females, and Hispanics, by far bear the brunt of the miscarriage of civil rights while white females are most often the trump card and primary benefactor of affirmative action policies.

Sometimes, it is standard procedure for supervisors to employ white females in significant numbers and use these statistics to justify their alleged support for the agencies affirmative action program. An unwritten but much adhered to policy is: if you have to pick a minority, choose a white female. Meanwhile, blacks and other minorities languish in the ranks of the under-represented.

Evasive discrimination barriers operate against upward mobility into the higher echelons of management and saps the morale and productivity of minority government personnel. These cases of continued employment discrimination practices at military installations are not voices of disgruntled employees who merely want a handout, but are real and unabashedly detailed factual accounts, where hard working people are routinely denied equal employment opportunity.

This cancer must be eradicated. However, before it can be dealt with it must be totally identified.

CHAPTER 7

Shh...Discrimination Is a Secret at the NSA

T he arms of discrimination reach into unseen corners of the government bureaucracy. Though it may seem invisible or appear to be nonexistent, it is exposed under close scrutiny and found covered beneath covert barriers of deceit.

An article published in the August 17, 1994, edition of *The Baltimore Sun* newspaper, reported that, "The National Security Agency (NSA), the nation's most secretive spy organization, has a secret of its own: one of the most dismal records in the Federal government for the hiring and promotion of minorities." The article went on to reveal that black workers feel they are "routinely bypassed for promotions."

A black analyst employed at the NSA was quoted as saying, "The numbers really speak for themselves. Management says they're trying to do something to change it. It's lip service. There's a problem out there and somebody has to look into this." Another analyst, a black female, remarked that she had been passed over for promotion at least a half dozen times and had been with the agency since the 1960's. Complaints were also expressed concerning the reluctance of management to put blacks in high visibility jobs and that the vast majority of black workers were in secretarial and clerical positions.

In response to these allegations, Michael A. Smith, NSA's Director of Policy, blamed its lack of minorities on "strenuous competition with other technical agencies and the private sector . . ." He went on to say that the agency would continue to "diversify our workforce through outreach programs" that would purportedly help minorities acquire the technical degrees and skills sought by NSA.

This is the consistent tune played by other federal agencies as well. Most every agency has programs supporting workforce diversity, but little success in diversifying, particularly when it comes to black representation. Why is it so hard for the Federal government to acquire competent black managers with all the programs touting their recruitment? The obvious reason is the halfhearted approach white managers take in honestly trying to recruit skilled black managers.

In a conversation I had with a GS-13 engineer, I asked why there were not more black engineers. His response was that whenever they went to college campuses, few black engineer majors would express interest in working for the Federal government. Puzzled, I further inquired as to what schools they were recruiting from and he cited Penn State as one example. My word of advice to him was if you want black engineers you need to go to black colleges. He appeared dumbfounded and stated that he never quite looked at it that way.

Another situation which displayed blatant ignorance or a callous disregard for the Federal government's programs of diversity recruitment was told to me by an EEO manager at the army installation I previously discussed in chapter 5. He conveyed that he was asked by white managers to accompany them on a trip to a black college. The purpose of the trip was to recruit black engineers, scientist and chemist.

When the EEO manager asked the white supervisors if they were prepared to offer jobs to interested graduates, they quickly declined saying they could not promise a job to anyone. The EEO manager refused the invitation because he was tired of supervisors visiting black colleges just to say for the record that they were making an attempt to adhere to diversity recruitment programs.

Even in the nontechnical fields blacks are rarely given intern positions while whites are recruited in earnest. When blacks are offered intern positions, many of them are forced to relocate geographically, while many whites are allowed to remain in their home state. For example, a black female intern was forced to move from Mississippi to Maryland before the government would hire her. When she arrived on her job she met many white interns who were from the immediate area.

Obviously, a person in familiar surroundings with family and friends available to support them will fare much better than a person who is in a foreign environment. Many black interns left the government because of discouragement and maladjustment based on the common scene described above. When a black intern leaves the government it has the effect of reinforcing in white supervisors minds that black employees are of a lower caliber then their white counterparts.

These defections make white supervisors reluctant to recruit blacks, and often times, are cited as reasons not to do so. The situation becomes a two edged sword. White managers are reluctant to hire blacks for managerial jobs, and blacks who do get hired are extremely frustrated by a system stacked against them. This frustration makes whites more reluctant to hire them.

Republicans from the Rush Limbaugh camp deny the existence of such exasperating predicaments when it comes to fairness in the work place. "Survival of the fittest" they scream. The problem with this theory is that whites primarily hire, promote, and award their own. They then use the statistical imbalance they created as proof of being the fittest.

In conclusion, clearly NSA has in place programs to promote diversity, but little to show in terms of their effectiveness. This is a problem which exist throughout the Federal government and has to be addressed before any substantial progress can be made in diversifying the workforce.

CHAPTER 8

The Federal Bureau of Investigation—and Discrimination

The Federal Bureau of Investigation (FBI) is unquestionably the most controversial government agency in relation to its policies affecting the black populace. As recorded, the Hoover years were notorious in its operations against the perceived threat of an emerging black leadership. Therefore, it comes as no surprise that racial discrimination takes center stage in FBI personnel practices.

In an article entitled, "FBI Agents Oppose Bias Settlement," published in the *Federal Times*, May 24, 1993, Leigh Rivenbark reports that the FBI Agents Association decided to oppose the provisions of a settlement agreement reached between the FBI and a group of black agents who had filed suit against the agency for its racially discriminatory personnel practices.

The agreement was an attempt to stave off a potential racial discrimination lawsuit. Under the terms of the agreement the FBI would have to do the following:

- Hire outside consultants to recommend changes in hiring, disciplinary procedures and performance methods;
- Allow all employees access to their personnel files (According to a spokesperson for the black agents, employees must file Freedom of Information Act request to see their own files.);
- Change methods for selecting agents for special assignments such as SWAT and hostage teams;
- Reserve specific promotions for black agents, including six supervisory positions and 13 "principle relief supervisory positions";
- Open 15 training slots for black agents, move five agents to primary SWAT teams and give additional training to others.

In light of the above settlement the FBI clearly realized discrimination existed within its agency. This constitutes a bonafide attempt by the FBI to put in place an affirmative action program that would assist in developing some form of parity within the organization.

At the time the article was written, only 500 of the FBI's 10,000 agents were black. This equates to less than 1 percent of the agent workforce. In spite of this huge disparity, where white men are predominate, the FBI Agents Association moved to block the implementation of the agency's settlement. The association asserted that the settlement violates equal employment rights of agents who are not black. They believe that since the FBI never admitted any racial discrimination, and no court ever ruled that discrimination did take place, the FBI is illegally giving black agents promotions and a stronger voice in changing policy and training.

The Association's comment was that the FBI ". . . cannot choose to accept input from some employees because they are black, and decline input from some employees because they are not. These provisions contemplate sweeping changes in virtually all aspects of the FBI's personnel practices and policies and will affect all FBI agents, yet under the proposed settlement agreement, only black FBI agents will be afforded any say in the development of new policies."

And further, according to the FBI Agents Association, black agents have the authority to pick one of the three members of the review committee which will comment on a proposal by outside experts, who will examine the FBI's personnel system. The association also says agents who are not black will not be afforded the same opportunity to select a member of the panel.

The attorney for the black agents said the FBI selects one member, the black agents' attorney selects one member, and a third is selected by the other two members. The attorney then went on to clarify that the person the black agents' attorney selects cannot be just anybody. They must be an expert industrial psychiatrist with experience in personnel systems.

Here again, a predominantly white organization uses the guise of alleged reverse-discrimination as a smoke screen to freeze in place a discriminatory system that benefits them. Contrarily, the reason the FBI came to an agreement with the black agents is because their concerns were being ignored and they were forced to resort to a lawsuit in order to be heard.

Once they were able to articulate their concerns and negotiate an agreement which would keep the FBI from totally excluding them in terms of promotions, training, and hiring, the FBI Agents Association decided to cry foul.

If there was any foul play involved it was on the part of the association, which takes credit for having all types of ethnic groups in its membership, but was reluctant to serve as a voice for the black agents who did not feel they were getting a fair shake from the FBI's personnel system. Instead, they decided to be a stumbling block against minority members in an attempt to protect the interest of their majority white male membership.

This is the common and sad dilemma facing black employees who work for the Federal government. They are forced to make the system respond to their concerns by engaging in costly and time consuming litigation. This process leaves them stigmatized and suggests that they can only make it if they are given preferential treatment.

Meanwhile, the majority (white males) continue to enjoy the benefit of "preferential treatment" while simultaneously using it as a weapon against the aspiring minority. Let's now take a look at another agency which employs agents who have sworn to uphold the sacred laws of our land—The Department of Immigration and Naturalization Services.

CHAPTER 9

The Borders of Racial Justice Are Closed at Immigration

One of the largest EEO cases ever leveled against a federal agency was reported in an article published in the *Federal Times*, March 14, 1994. The case centered around the under-representation of blacks in the Immigration and Naturalization Service (INS). Leigh Rivenbark, the staff writer responsible for the article, disclosed that this case involved over 500 black employees nationwide with the possibility of this number doubling to over 1,000. This under-representation is based upon the following statistics:

- Of the 4,045 Border Patrol agents in 1993 only 42 or more appropriately, 1 percent were black. Outside of government, 11.4 percent of people in similar occupations were black;

- In the total officer corps employees, 3.6 percent, or 56 of the 1,553 supervisors were black;

- There were no blacks in Senior Executive Service

or GM-15 officer corps positions. The number of black managers in non-officer corps jobs far exceeded their numbers in the officer corps;

• Hiring over the past six years has remained flat, with no real increases in the number of blacks hired.

Further statistics revealed the following: Among Border Patrol agents 1 percent were black in 1987 and 1 percent in 1993; among Special agents 5.2 percent were black in 1987 and 5.1 percent in 1993; and among the Inspectors staff 9.6 percent in 1987, the same percentage in 1993.

These statistics were so disheartening they prompted one black senior special agent to write Congress and comment that, "Black employees are no more than high-profile, modern day slaves of this government." It was further reported that black employees who filed the class action are hoping the case serves as a "wake up call" to the Federal government.

It was also stated that blacks in INS feel betrayed because in their view, Congress cares more about foreign nationals than about them. The attorney for the black agents, David Ross, estimated the cost to the Federal government in the final outcome of this case could be in the area of $50 million.

This real but allusive reality is everything that the government should fight against, namely bigotry and racial injustice. Probably the most criminal component of this obtrusive behavior is that the INS will potentially make taxpayers liable for $50 million. This figure only takes into account the potential compensatory damages the Federal government would have to pay.

Regardless of what the final taxpayer bill is, chances are that not one senior level official at INS will be reprimanded for the perpetuated practice of racial exclusion. This provides no deterrent to change their behavior, and the Federal government will continue to treat the symptoms while the root causes remain untreated.

It is absurd that an agency of the Federal government could be so blatantly apathetic towards the imbalance between black employees and their white counterparts. In the medical community, a flat line on a patient's vital signs signify the person is in cardiac arrest. The same could be said for the "flat line" that has existed for six years in this agency's hiring of qualified black employees.

The INS is definitely in cardiac arrest on the issue of equal employment opportunity. Speaking of symptoms, the next agency we will examine specializes in understanding what symptoms could lead to. It is the Center for Disease Control and Prevention located in Atlanta, Georgia.

CHAPTER 10

A Disease Out of Control

W hile it is apparent that the disease of discrimination exists in the federal workforce, it cunningly evades detection by the government agency responsible for identifying and controlling the spread of infectious germs, and continues to thrive in an environment conducive to the perpetuation of its existence. This affliction remains unchecked and uncontrolled.

In an article published in the *Federal Times*, Christy Harris, a staff writer for the publication, reported that black employees at the Center for Disease Control (CDC) charged that the agency discriminated in hiring, training and promotions. Three CDC employees moved to have a judge grant them class action status so they could represent 620 non-supervisory black employees against the Department of Health and Human Services.

One of the employees wanting to represent the

class disclosed that he had applied for 25 promotions over a two year period, but lost out to white males each time. Currently a GS-12, he believes he would be a GS-14 if the CDC did not discriminate.

The class action lawsuit alleged that a predominantly white supervisory workforce hired blacks at lower grades than their white counterparts and that blacks are also denied training opportunities and promotions at a greater frequency than whites. One of the complainants, a GS-7 biologist, was hired as a GS-4 lab technician. He alleges that white applicants with similar qualifications were hired at higher grades. He goes on to say that, "There are clear cut examples of some of the racist practices. This type of blackballing of minorities is quite common and endemic within all of CDC."

Another complainant went so far as to quit because he was being harassed. He testified that, "During my employment, I have sought promotions on many occasions without success. Blacks are often put into dead-end positions with no chance to advance." The complainants are asking for $60 million in compensatory damages, retroactive promotions, back pay, and the institution of an effective affirmative action plan.

The chairman of a task force studying diversity issues at CDC was quoted as saying, "We already have a diverse workforce." Yet, he went on to say that, "There are areas where we need to be more diverse" and further believes the agency should focus on retention of minorities instead of recruiting. The comments made by the head of the task force are typical of how government agencies try to over-simplify the problems encountered by minorities.

Even though the CDC is facing a lawsuit of $60 million in compensatory damages alone, they choose to classify the situation as a retention problem. This is almost laughable if it weren't so tragic. The reason why the CDC can't retain minorities is because minorities don't believe they have an opportunity for advancement. If the agency is not prepared to remedy this situation, they can't possibly hope to retain them. It is the proverbial catch twenty-two.

Oversimplification of discrimination allegations are not unique to the Federal government in general. This is one of the reasons discrimination goes on unchecked. It can be reasoned that every EEO investigator operates under an unwritten mandate which says that the finding of discrimination is a last resort.

Tragically, the current judicial climate supports this mandate by not putting the burden of proof on employers to give legitimate nondiscriminatory reasons for gross statistical imbalances. With this kind of justice prevailing, the employer boldly stands behind the system and dares the complainants to prove discrimination. This is why many minorities fall victim to the callousness with which supervisors discriminate.

My personal experience with the Federal government is that it commonly and consistently trivializes most instances of discrimination by saying there was a lack of communication or a misunderstanding. This message tells the complainant that their charges of discrimination are imaginary, or at most petty, and in essence, tells the employer to be a more effective communicator. Neither of these messages solve the underlying problems which lead to allegations of racial discrimination such as those at the CDC.

Minorities are continually thwarted in their attempt to show they are being denied basic opportunities that white employees (particularly white males) take for granted. The Equal Employment Opportunity Commission is in effect saying, okay, we see the facts and you are being denied, but until we see pictures of Klansmen in your office yelling racial epithets, we can't be sure its racially motivated. When you tell this to an employee who has applied for 25 promotions over two years and each time was passed over for the preferred white male, it becomes obvious that the government is defaulting on its constitutional obligation to ensure equal opportunity for all.

CHAPTER 11

Agriculture:
The Last Plantation

In the time of slavery, a life sentence on the plantation meant backbreaking labor from dawn to dusk without just compensation. Many blacks spent their lives working the fields to produce wealth for the plantation owner who prospered from the institutionalized privilege of free labor. Residue of this practice remains embedded in the personnel system of the Federal government where minority employees, particularly blacks, are systematically denied equal compensation and fair opportunity for advancement. Ironically, this system of racial discrimination continues to exist in the Department of Agriculture (USDA), infamously known as the "last plantation."

An article published in the October 31, 1994, edition of the *Federal Times*, Meg Walker, a staff writer, reported that the USDA was referred to as the "last plantation" because of the number of discrimination complaints filed by its minority employees. It was revealed that things are so bad that blacks formed a new organization within USDA called The Coalition of Minority Employees (aka, The Coalition). Asian-Americans, Hispanics, womens' groups, and employees with disabilities also joined the fight. (It must be noted here that the formation of The Coalition serves as a model that has the potential to spread beyond the confines of USDA and become a platform through which all minorities in the Federal government can speak in one forceful voice.)

The leader of the Asian group found it very difficult to get management at USDA to recognize that the agency has a "glass ceiling" which minority employees cannot penetrate. He was quoted as saying, "We've met with administrators to see how to rectify a lot of problems," and he further stated that, "The result was just meetings, and then everything goes on its merry way. The basic concern I have is the old boy network. Agriculture has its own culture."

Further noted, the Office of Civil Rights Enforcement conducted a survey within USDA and found that among the Asian-American respondents, 251 had doctorate degrees, 157 had masters degrees, and 383 had bachelor's degrees. Of these 791 respondents, only 79 were in grades 14 or 15 and none were career senior executives.

In addition, 129 were in grade 13, 221 in grade 12, and those who had bachelor's degrees were primarily in grades below GS-11. The report concluded that, "If career advancement is contingent on educational achievement, more Asian-American employees should be in the senior positions than the current 2.1 percent in USDA." Here is a situation where a minority group (Asian-Americans) has an extremely high educational profile and yet they still cannot penetrate the "glass ceiling."

Lawrence Lucas, spokesperson for The Coalition expressed similar concerns in pointing out that of the 356 senior executive positions only nine were black. He was also very disturbed with the way the EEO system was administered at USDA. According to him, the system was ineffective in resolving complaints primarily because it takes so long.

The Coalition attempted to circumvent the EEO process by taking its concerns directly to then Secretary Mike Espy. At this meeting they presented Secretary Espy with a list of problems confronted by minorities which included recommendations for improvement; as follows:

- Agency heads should submit written reports describing how discrimination complaints have been resolved for the last two years. If disparities were found, they wanted Secretary Espy to issue guidelines on settling complaints;
- Managers should be suspended for retaliating against employees who have filed discrimination or other complaints;

- Managers should be penalized for failing to nominate minorities along with other employees to serve on various task forces;
- The secretary should issue a policy which warned managers against pre-selecting job candidates. The policy should make it clear that if a manager violates this order, they will be punished.
- A task force on recruitment should be created and include Coalition representatives.

Tragically, Secretary Espy was pressured to resign prior to acting on these suggested initiatives. The Coalition was deeply disturbed and immediately fired off a letter to the President of the United States in which they essentially wrote, "Mr. President, we believe Secretary Espy deserved the opportunity to continue leading USDA toward accomplishing the goals and objectives of your administration and those he has articulated for USDA."

Not only was it an anomaly that USDA was headed by a minority, it was also uncharacteristic to see this minority actively trying to correct the situation. This may come as a surprise to many, but very seldom will minorities, particularly blacks, who are in high positions, help those aspiring to get ahead. The similarities between the psychology of blacks in the days of slavery and the psychology of blacks in the workforce today are sometimes uncanny.

In the days of slavery, house slaves and overseers

were primarily interested in sustaining their small edge in life and had no desire to help the plight of those who were less fortunate. This narrow minded view is still in existence today. One could rationalize this type of thinking under the system of slavery because blacks had no rights and could be beaten, killed, or sold away at the masters' whim.

One would think that in today's time of civil rights that black managers would be very receptive to insuring qualified blacks were hired and promoted at every opportunity. To the contrary, many black employees dread working for black supervisors. Oftentimes, black managers are tougher on their black employees and go out of their way to make it known. It's as if they are stigmatized and fear white males scrutinizing their every move, waiting for them to give even the slightest hint of favoritism towards other blacks.

As in the days of human bondage, black managers are deathly afraid that their careers will suffer if they do not conform to the discrimination policies of their white counterparts and maintain their vote of confidence by being the proverbial "house slave." Most of them are more common to operate in the mold of a Clarence Thomas versus a Mike Espy.

Somehow the opponents of affirmative action constantly harp about how corrective measures designed to promote equal opportunity are nothing more than established quotas that erode the talent of the workforce because it forces supervisors to hire inferior workers.

This is a myth and a con job the American public has bought lock, stock and barrel. It is obvious that the "glass ceiling" is the culprit that robs our country of a wealth of genius and a bevy of talented minorities who are being held hostage to the vicious barriers of discrimination.

In conclusion, whether former Secretary Espy committed improprieties that violated the public trust may never be known. But to the minorities at USDA, his resignation will always be associated with a "political lynching" that is indicative of business as usual on the "last plantation."

CHAPTER 12

Discrimination Is Big Business at Commerce

C apitalism, the symbol of freedom in the New World, established its roots in the commerce of black gold stripped from a mine abundant with human flesh. The forceful immigration of Africans was the bedrock that allowed growth and the creation of an economically viable society independent of British rule.

They were the cornerstone that served as the foundation of the American colonies' success in gaining independence and separation from the authority of the royal crown. This piggyback practice continues to be used even today to underwrite a discriminatory system fraught with white dominance of power and control.

In an article entitled, "Black Workers Bash Commerce for Bias," published in the June 13, 1994, edition of the *Federal Times*, Leigh Rivenbark reported that an organization known as the Commerce Committee for

African-American Concerns, accused the Department of Commerce of having a "plantation mentality." In addition, it was revealed that the employees at Commerce were totally disenchanted with the EEO complaint process. The EEO complaints were taking up to a year on average to be settled even though the law requires agencies to make a decision on these complaints within 80 days!

In an open letter to the late Secretary Ron Brown, the employees reported that blacks encounter a "deplorable working environment" involving retaliation when they formally file complaints outlining their grievances. This retaliation surfaces in performance evaluations, awards, and promotions according to a consensus of the group in evaluating their collective experiences at Commerce.

In order to get their point across, representatives of the NAACP along with hundreds of Commerce employees, conducted a demonstration protesting the alleged racism at the agency. It was revealed that of the 33,000 employees at Commerce, blacks comprise 18 percent, yet make up less than 7 percent of the professional workforce. The Committee for African-American Concerns accused the agency of not promoting blacks by predetermining their selection and in some cases, canceling vacancies if they cannot hire who they want.

During the protest, employees carried signs reading "Promotion possibilities should be color blind; The

Commerce EEO office is a mockery"; and "We train them and in a few years, they supervise us." The employee group gave the late Secretary Brown specific recommendations to remedy the situation. They asked him to remove the EEO director; establish EEO as a critical requirement in supervisory evaluations; and that they want an agency ombudsman appointed for EEO.

After reviewing the situation at Commerce, it appeared that Secretary Brown was genuinely concerned about the allegations of racism within his department. Yet, one would question his methodology in dealing with this issue. The article reported that his response was to appoint four working groups to review EEO, employee training, advancement, recruitment, and performance appraisals. One of the representatives of the NAACP summed up this reaction best by saying, "We don't need any more working groups, we don't need any more studies. We don't need to waste any more time."

This whole idea of studies and working groups has become nothing more than a Tower of Babel—a whole lot of work and nothing to show for it. The minority employees are fed up with the government's proclivity to convene a task force or commission a study. Regrettably, the leadership at Commerce fell into the same old standard along with other government officials of "looking into the matter."

It is evident that the Department of Commerce is an organization that is engaged in violating the civil rights of thousands of capable, qualified, and energetic employees who only want to be afforded the same opportunities as their white counterparts.

The last agency we will look at is the Equal Employment Opportunity Commission (EEOC). The EEOC is the entity charged with investigating discrimination complaints for the government. In many of the departments previously looked at, employees expressed no confidence in the EEOC to fairly and expeditiously adjudicate their complaint. Let's see why.

CHAPTER 13

If You Want to Win at the EEOC, Produce Photographs of a Lynching

Although the existence and practice of racial discrimination in the personnel system of the Federal government has long been acknowledged, it remains to be an elusive source of confusion, frustration, and denial. While the elements of proof required to establish the presence and application of racial discrimination fluctuate with the hands of time, it remains constant and potent in its effect and purpose.

Evidence presented by complainants who allege that their rights were violated because of racial bias, must essentially be exposed on prime time television in order for the charges to be considered credible. And even then, it's likely that the broadcast will be rated as an episode of fiction with a trailing qualifier that the story is a product of the complainants imagination— and that names, places, and dates were changed to protect the guilty.

An article published in the August 8, 1993, edition of the *Federal Times*, by staff writer Ken Hughes reported that the Equal Employment Opportunity Commission (EEOC), the agency charged with enforcing the administration of fair employment practices, processed 68,000 discrimination complaints in 1992. Yet, a finding of discrimination occurred in only 2.4 percent of these complaints. This means, assuming the EEOC was correct in its findings, that 66,368 government employees were incorrect in categorizing their problem as discrimination.

In fairness to the agency, it was reported that 40 percent of these complaints were reconciled or withdrawn for various reasons. That means a whooping 60 percent were closed because it was decided that there was not enough evidence to support a finding of discrimination. It was furthered revealed by a number of EEOC investigators that because of the volume of complaints handled by the agency, they prematurely closed cases to avoid having their performance ratings adversely impacted for missing deadlines. In a previous report, the General Accounting Office (GAO), which monitors and audits the operations of Federal government agencies, expressed concern about the increased workload causing EEOC investigators to close cases prematurely.

As noted, the major concern of GAO is the effect of the mounting case load on EEOC investigators, yet sadly, this situation will not improve in the foreseeable future primarily due to the economic and political climate in which the government is now operating. The result is that the processing of cases takes even longer as the case backlog increases the length of time to complete each one.

The GAO estimated that the average age of the cases handled by the EEOC would rise from 10 months to 21 months by 1994. A complainant can expect to wait close to two years for EEOC to rule on their case. And even then, if by some stroke of luck there is a finding of discrimination, the agency involved will more than likely reject it, further prolonging the process.

According to a spokesperson for the Washington Lawyers Committee on Civil Rights, an agency can reject the findings of the EEOC for whatever reason it chooses, and in many cases for no reason at all. In 1991, 68.4 percent of discrimination findings were rejected by the agency involved.

While a complainant waits on the EEOC to render a ruling on their case, they are oftentimes subjected to retaliatory actions by management which causes additional cases to be filed in reprisal. The results of this vicious spiral is a tragedy for the employee, management, the EEOC, and ultimately the taxpayer. The employee becomes disgruntled and unproductive, management becomes vindictive, the EEOC continues to operate minus the resources and commitment to bring about a lasting truce, and the taxpayer bears the cost of this perpetual cycle of shame.

Surprisingly, one member of elected leadership, Senator Paul Simon, recognizes that the EEOC needs to be shaken up. In the October 31,1994, edition of the *Federal Employees News Digest*, Senator Simon was quoted as saying to the EEOC Chairman Gilbert Casellas, that "employees who do not believe in the mission of the EEOC . . . be transferred to the Pentagon or someplace else." The Senator touched on a major problem that is a permanent deterrent of the EEOC in doing its job.

There are undoubtedly many employees at the EEOC who do not believe in its mission. These unbelievers receive pay at taxpayers expense while they continue to undermine the public trust and the authority delegated to the agency to enforce equal treatment of all government employees. This attitude of internal subversion flourished during the Clarence Thomas regime at EEOC and continues unabated.

Even in the face of overwhelming evidence to the contrary, Republicans like Clarence Thomas cling to the belief that an employer will hire, promote, and discipline on a fair and equitable basis regardless of race. With this type of employee in its ranks, the EEOC will never be more than a catacomb in which complaints are stockpiled and buried.

The EEOC is a broken process which epitomizes all that is wrong with the Federal government. For the government to win back the trust and faith of the minority employees who are being injured, it must first get this inefficient monolith of a bureaucracy under control. Minorities working for the government are screaming for justice and equal opportunity. Yet, the EEOC, the agency chartered to discover viable solutions to this dilemma, has a dismal track record in resolving these disputes. This has caused minorities to have a negative image of the EEOC which ultimately affects the efficiency, production, and daily operation of the Federal government in serving the public at large. This is a self-destructive course that must be halted, lest the explosion be loud and clear, and the recourse far too late.

So far, we have introduced irrefutable evidence that the government is allowing discrimination to run rampant throughout its ranks. No one agency has a monopoly on this market, even though some are obviously more devious then others.

Now that we have laid out the preponderance of evidence where do we go from here? It won't do a bit of good to continue talking about what the government is allowing managers to do to thousands of hard working law abiding and tax paying employees. The government knows the facts are out there, and so do my republican colleagues who profess that white males are being treated unfairly.

Someone once said, "A man convinced against his will is unconvinced still." We must remember this when we engage the opponents of affirmative action in meaningful dialogue. Republicans will not be coerced into changing their stance on affirmative action. They have to be shown how workforce diversity is in America's best interest.

Let's now take a look at the kind of thinking which has contributed to the widespread discrimination we have already talked about. The infamous book, *The Bell Curve* epitomizes the true feelings of anti-affirmative action advocates.

CHAPTER 14

The Bell Curve and Those Who Believe in It

The controversial book *The Bell Curve*, by Charles Murray and Richard J. Herrnstein, is a tragic and chilling tale of a paranoid minority and their reaction to the emergence of a diverse global population where shifts of power are eminent. While the white populace listens intently to interpret the meaning of the bell's ding, its dong is curved to resonate a tone of confused panic, a wrenching sound of academic ignorance, and a vain attempt to scientifically rationalize unrational behavior.

By removing the facade of illusions erected by the architects of modern day racism, the underlying basis for understanding the practice of race discrimination in the Federal government is exposed. Without a doubt, *The Bell Curve* is one of the most racist books ever published. It is far more dangerous than anything white supremacist or the Ku Klux Klan (KKK) could ever print because it claims to scientifically validate what these extremist groups have always believed. By espousing that blacks are intellectually inferior, the authors attempt to confirm the pathetic notion of white superiority, while simultaneously attacking affirmative action as a futile policy.

Many whites, when sure of their company, reveal that they believe that blacks are intellectually deficient. They wholeheartedly embrace what Murray and Herrstein profess they have scientifically proven. The belief that whites are mentally superior is directly related to the reluctance of white Federal government managers to hire or promote qualified and deserving black candidates.

Because of this racial paradigm, white managers routinely discriminate while arbitrarily believing they have actually chosen the most qualified candidates. I can't count the number of times I have been in a meeting and experienced the blatant unwillingness of other managers to consider my input, or in some cases acknowledge my presence. In many cases my input resurfaced as a great idea out of some other manager's mouth. This is one of the most frustrating phenomenon's of being black in the Federal government.

Oftentimes, minorities are compelled to sit and listen to white men and women who obviously don't have a clue as to what's going on, and yet are unable to provide input simply because of their race. This has the effect of taking away the intellectual self-worth of thousands of black employees. This raping of the mind robs the government of a vast pool of human resources, that would be an invaluable asset in helping agencies survive in an era of declining budgets and high demand for value and quality.

In a *Newsweek* article entitled "IQ, Is It Destiny?" writer Tom Morganthau summarized the basic premises of *The Bell Curve* and outlined the three main arguments set forth by its authors Murray and Herrstein.

To begin, these two authors assert that America consists of three levels of intellect. Accordingly, the ruling class is made up of what they term the cognitive elite which is overwhelmingly made up of white males. They maintain that these are the people that have high IQ's, attend prestigious universities, invariably run the country as heads of corporations, and become leaders of government, academia, etc.

The next cognitive group is the middle class and although they are the largest segment of this intellectual hierarchy, they remain virtually irrelevant and not discussed by the authors. At the bottom of this pool are the intellectually inferior underclass, termed the cognitive disadvantaged, who they determine cannot rise up the socioeconomic ladder because they lack the cognitive capacity to do so.

Murray and Herrstein believe that mental deficiency is the reason these people, the vast majority being black, are destined to live a life of violence, teenage pregnancy, poverty, and welfare dependency. If one accepts their belief that blacks have a second rate gene pool, it's easy to justify excluding them from mainstream America. *The Bell Curve* is based on so-called scientific data. However, this data is questionable when one truly considers the value of biased standardized tests which purportedly measure a person's intellect.

Nonetheless, the authors rely upon these standardized tests and conclude that blacks are a lower mental species than whites. This is the ultimate message of *The Bell Curve*. It espouses thoughts, under the guise of erroneous scientific data, that rationalizes the practice of racial discrimination. Its scathing attack on affirmative action is born out of the absurd belief that blacks are not qualified to compete with whites.

Yet, in the vast majority of discrimination cases, blacks are more qualified than the whites who get the jobs or promotions. Any attempt to condone discrimination or perpetuate a false confidence of superiority based on racial difference is bigotry, counterproductive, and outright stupid. Of most importance, it is a dangerous and unhealthy seed to plant in the fertile ground of mental development in white children.

The *Newsweek* article states that Murray and Herrstein, ". . . insist that whites and blacks alike must face up to the reality of black intellectual disadvantage. The authors further conclude that, 'We cannot think of a legitimate argument why . . . whites and blacks need be affected by the knowledge that an aggregate difference in measured intelligence is genetic instead of environmental." This is the most preposterous and outlandish comment made by these authors.

They somehow believe this information should have no bearing on how blacks and whites view each other. Who are they trying to fool? The root cause of racial discrimination is directly linked to this perceived mental superiority, particularly on the part of white males. It is obvious how they will react once they hear science has once again tried to erroneously confirm their racist beliefs.

A question: Who is more at fault, the welfare recipient or the welfare creator? I heard Jack Kemp, a republican colleague I highly respect say, "If you subsidize something you get more of it. If you tax something, you get less of it." This country has been subsidizing debt, laziness, promiscuity, drug dependency, and other vices which ultimately destroy a society. Simultaneously, we have taxed productivity, creativity, entrepreneurship, and other solid foundations upon which a society must be built.

The net effect is that we have gotten more of what we don't want and less of what we should want. I have often asked the question that if an individual chooses to get free food, free medical care, and virtually free housing versus working for minimum wage and no benefits, are they really lazy and no good or are they just making an intelligent business decision?

Much of America's ills are the product of the so-called cognitive elite. In fact, the problems in America, highlighted by massive deficit spending, are not the product of the cognitive disadvantaged underclass as *The Bell Curve* purports, but are the problems created and sustained by this cognitive elite. Following is a list that chronicles major blunders of the cognitive elite which decisively dispel the mythical belief of white mental superiority:

• The massive loss of market share by IBM was a result of their cognitive elite leadership failing to react to the changing face of the computer industry. Years before Microsoft ever came on the scene it was obvious that software and smaller computers with increased power would eventually dominate the market. In spite of all the indicators and having more resources than any competitor, IBM refused to deviate from making main frames their primary business. Net result was billions of dollars in losses, and close to 200,000 people laid off.

• Apple Computer and their cognitive elite decided that they would never license their extremely user friendly operating system. The CEO stated in the 1994 edition of *Fortune* magazine, that it was one of the dumbest business decisions the world has ever seen. Bill Gates makes some variations to the Apple concept and creates Windows. Net result was 80% of the world's computers now use Windows or DOS as their operating system. Apple never recovers and is relegated to having a great operating system with very little market share.

• In 1984 when AT&T was forced to divest in local phone companies its cognitive elite threw away a golden opportunity to become the leader in a new market of cellular telephones. Instead of taking advantage of this untapped market they decided there would be less then 1 million cellular users by 1995. In their minds this was hardly a market worth pursuing. In one of the biggest miscalculations of all times, AT&T stood on the sidelines while 20 million people signed up to use cellular phones. By the time AT&T decided to play, they were so far behind they had to go the acquisition route. Total cost of this blunder was $12 billion. That was the price they paid to acquire McCaw Cellular (as reported in December 12, 1994, edition of *Fortune* magazine).

• Massive deficit spending is another brain child of the cognitive elite. Every household knows you can't indefinitely spend more than your income or eventually you will become bankrupt. The newest versions of the cognitive elite residing over the nation's affairs have promised to balance the budget in 7 years, enact a middle class tax cut, and not touch Social Security which amounts to approximately 50% of the budget. Net result will probably be the bankruptcy of America, a worldwide depression, and millions of people plunged into poverty.

As clearly shown, the cognitive elite made major blunders which continue to have a tremendous negative impact on the lives of hundreds of thousands of people. These examples prove that while IQ tests may measure aggregate intelligence, it in no way measures how people will function in real world situations.

The Bell Curve was based on so-called scientific data. However, this data is questionable when one really considers the value of standardized tests which reportedly measure a persons intelligence level. Nonetheless, the authors have their "gods of science" they rely upon, and with their guidance they concluded that blacks are without a doubt a lower mental species than whites. Having said this, let me now turn to the Bible to refute their conclusion and expose their fraudulent message.

First, let's look at the argument that blacks are an inferior genetic species. In the book of Genesis, chapter 10:1, God identifies the three sons of Noah. This is significant because it clearly tells us that all mankind came from Noah after the flood. The three sons were Shem, Ham and Japheth. Historical biblical research has shown that Shem was the father of the Jews, Jepheth was the father of the whites and people of European origin, and Ham was the father of the blacks.

The Bible further states, in verses 6 through 10, that Ham had a son name Cush and he had a son name Nimrod. In verse 8, God identifies Nimrod as being "a mighty one in the earth." Verse 10 lists the original localities of his kingdom. "And the beginning of his kingdom was Babel, and E-rech, and Ac-cad, and Cal-neh, in the land of Shinar." Knowing that most people are familiar with the story of the Tower of Babel, let's take a closer look at this part of Nimrod's Kingdom.

Genesis 11:1 tells us that during this time, the world ". . . was of one language, and of one speech." The people traveled east and settled in Shinar, a part of Nimrod's kingdom. Apparently under Nimrod's tutelage the people decided to build the infamous tower of Babel. The goal of this incredible engineering project was to reach heaven (Genesis 11:4). As ludicrous as this may seem to the average unbeliever, verses 5 through 9 says that the Lord Himself came down to see this project, and proclaimed the project as being possible.

> "And the Lord said, Behold, the people is one, and they have all one language; and this they begin to do: and now nothing will be restrained from them, which they have imagined to do."

The Lord then confused their language causing them not to be able to understand one another. This aborted the project and effectively scattered the people throughout the earth as God had intended for them to do.

Okay, by now you're asking, "What has this to do with dispelling the notion of blacks being inferior genetically?" As I have already discussed, *The Bell Curve* identifies inferior genetics as the primary cause of blacks having a low IQ. But the Word of God explicitly credits a black man with reigning over the first one world government after the flood. Although I do not take pride in this government because of how they disobeyed God's commandment to scatter across the face of the earth, it certainly is apparent that this massive undertaking could not have been led by a mentally inferior human being. Nimrod must have been a highly intellectual person to have galvanized all people in one mind-set, for the purpose of building a tower that could reach heaven.

The tower was so intricately designed and architecturally brilliant that God himself affirmed it's possibility. So the black inferior gene could not have started at this early point of human history now could it?

An even more satisfying revelation turns up in the book of Matthew chapter 1:5. A lady by the name of Ruth, who was a Moabite, is named in the genealogy of our Lord and Savior Jesus Christ! Moabites were also descendants of Ham; therefore Jesus himself was a recipient of this so-called inferior gene pool. This soundly refutes the notion of blacks having inferior genetics.

I'm not bringing these facts out so that blacks can boast. After all, it is only our Great God and Creator Jesus Christ who made our forefathers the highly intelligent human beings they were.

God is no respecter of persons (Acts 10:34). He did not create any one race of people genetically superior to another, and any attempt on the part of science to prove otherwise is a fraudulent message instigated by Satan, God's enemy. It's an attempt to deceive and divide the people so that hatred and bigotry can rule the hearts of men.

The Bell Curve is racism at its best. Yet, it offers a basis for understanding the underlying and root cause for rampant racial discrimination in the Federal government. It is essentially a sad story of a vain and feeble attempt to preserve a legacy of racial preference and privilege through the institution of white supremacy.

CHAPTER 15

A Blue Print for Change

The time has come where it is paramount and of extreme urgency that the chapters of racial discrimination and biased employment practices in the Federal government come to a close. The practice of employment unfairness is based on the concept of racial exclusion where the value of minority employee participation is underrated or simply ignored. Subsequently, this abundant and valuable resource of diversity remains dormant and untapped by the agents entrusted to manage the federal bureaucracy.

However, fairness and equality in the federal workforce can be achieved, yet, it cannot come without sincere commitment, coupled with a valid program for reeducation, and anchored in honest dialogue dealing with the concerns of minority employees and the fears of predominantly white male managers. It is imperative that the Federal government explore and institute viable solutions to remedy this self-imposed paralysis which essentially impedes its overall effectiveness in honoring its constitutional commission to ensure equal opportunity for all.

In an article entitled "How to Make Diversity Pay" in *Fortune* magazine, Faye Rice issued a report on companies that were successful in making diversity a positive asset for both the employee and employer. Of all the companies identified, (IBM and AT&T included), the star company that emerged as the shining example in discovering and implementing policies that utilize the wealth of its diverse workforce was the chemical conglomerate Hoechst Celanese.

It was revealed that the visionary behind this company's innovative solutions in identifying and managing the hidden wealth of employee diversity is its Chief Executive Officer (CEO), Earnest H. Drew. In the article, Mr. Drew disclosed that the value of diversity was revealed to him while attending a conference that was attended by primarily white men and a small number of lower ranking women and minorities.

According to his account of the conference, the participates were divided into problem solving teams where some were integrated by race and sex, while others were made up of mostly white males. The purpose of this exercise as contended by Mr. Drew, was to look at "how the corporate culture affected the business and what changes might be made to improve results." When the teams submitted their ideas Mr.

Drew was astounded to find that the more diverse teams presented the most innovative solutions.

This revelation prompted him to state that, "It was so obvious that the diverse teams had the broader solutions . . . They had ideas I hadn't even thought of. For the first time we realized that diversity is a strength as it relates to problem solving. Before, we just thought of diversity as the total number of minorities and women in the company, like affirmative action. Now we know we need diversity at every level of the company where decisions are made."

This realization of the advantage and benefit of diversity in the workforce must be broadcast throughout Congress and Federal government agencies. It stands in direct contradiction to *The Bell Curve* and the contention that affirmative action weakens the quality of our workforce.

Diversity is a positive asset to be courted and utilized. If racial bias can be discarded the Federal government would uncover an immeasurable treasure of culturally diverse input within its minority workforce. Accordingly, the prerequisite for the emergence of these ideals must be an environment that is fair and committed in properly acknowledging and rewarding the minorities who give birth to them.

In the *Fortune* article, the following lessons were cited as critical to any company's success in managing diversity as a business asset:

• Get the CEO's commitment. In the Federal government the commitment must start with the President, travel through Congress, and ultimately find its way into every government agency. The President must push diversity with evangelistic fervor. He must understand how diversity adds to the business of government and push this philosophy down to the lowest possible level.

President Clinton has done a better job than his republican predecessors, but the emphasis on diversity is still nothing more then window dressing. The current Congress has shown no desire to make it a priority at all. The policy of white males first and forever is not going to allow our government to successfully navigate the challenges of a global community presence. Neither would a policy of black males only, white females only, or any other race monopoly be effective or desired. If no man is an island unto himself, then no single race is either.

No longer can the Commander and Chief allow managers to espouse the racist precepts described in *The Bell Curve*. Blacks and other minorities must be treated with dignity and respect. They cannot be viewed as miscreants who were only hired to satisfy affirmative action goals. To the contrary, blacks have real contributions to make and relish the opportunity to be judged on merit.

It can be reasonably ascertained that the primary reason blacks and other minorities are pro-affirmative action is because the majority of white managers have shown no eagerness to hire, promote, or award qualified and deserving minorities.

Case in point: A black female budget analyst, working on an army installation in the northern suburbs of Baltimore was responsible for seven different programs in her office. During this time she was at the grade of GS-11. After experiencing blatant discrimination and subsequently getting a new job, her former office divided her duties among three white employees who were then promoted to the GS-12 grade. To eradicate situations like these the President must make fair and effective management of diversity a high priority. Whenever the playing field is truly level, minorities will more than likely be the first to advocate the abolition of affirmative action.

• **Make diversity a business objective.** At Hoechst Celanese, workforce diversity is one of the primary performance criteria in determining manager salaries. By tying diversity to their pay, managers were more than willing to participate.

In the same *Fortune* article, Mr. Drew gave an additional example of the business value inherent in diversity. He emphasized that industrial plants that had a diverse workforce were experiencing a rise in productivity. One significant experience cited involved his polyester filament textile division. It had been losing money for 18 consecutive years and in the late 1980's launched a major effort to recruit minorities and women.

According to Mr. Drew, "Under the leadership of Grover Smith, an African-American who was then the director of polyester filament production, and his diverse business team of women, white males, and people of color, polyester filament began to turn around. The teams winning strategy was to de-emphasize what had always been seen as the division's core business, commodity production. Instead the team cut cost, improved quality, and concentrated on niche markets such as automotive upholstery. The filament division pulled into the black in 1992 and posted a substantial profit in 1993 . . ."

Testimonials such as these, are proof positive that diversity of personnel adds value to companies wise enough to realize and properly manage it as they would any other asset. The government needs to make diversity a business objective which would add value to the myriad of tasks in which Uncle Sam is involved in. The people the government serves are diversified and its workforce should reflect that diversity.

Affirmative action plans and goals are perceived as negative in the eyes of most Americans. Business objectives, however, are not. By putting these objectives in the evaluations of all managers and rigorously enforcing adherence, the government would make a positive step towards re-educating its managers in the value and necessity of diversity.

• **Adopt a plan to address concerns of white males.** Of all the lessons learned by companies who made the commitment to properly manage diversity, it was found that white males are vehemently against affirmative action or any other program which advocates diversity primarily because they feel as though they are the odd man out. Their feelings are probably no different than what any other racial group would feel if suddenly the government enacted policies to hire more employees from cultures different then theirs. This would make anybody feel insecure and believe they are a victim of reverse-discrimination.

In order to deal with these phobias the government must educate white males on the value of diversity and more importantly make clear where they fit into this equation. Some companies are conducting training classes to help white males deal with this issue and the loss of the world they knew. The government could conduct these classes and allow white males to talk about their concerns as well as educate them on managing diversity in their organizations.

While it is true that many EEO offices conduct training, much of this training centers on the minority perspective and leaves white males feeling even more alienated. These classes must be re-engineered to properly address white male fears and concerns. If the government is ever going to seriously make diversity a priority, white males must be made to feel an essential part of the plan.

• **Scrutinize compensation and career tracking for fairness.** Addressing the issue of fairness in pay is critical. If the government wants minorities to believe it is serious about treating people fairly, then "just compensation" has to be pursued. There are many minorities, particularly blacks, who are routinely paid less than their counterparts.

As an example, Hoechst Celanese implemented standard reviews of compensation. These reviews were established to identify disparities in salary not related to performance or longevity. The initial review of employee compensation in 1992 revealed a disparity between white males and minorities. This disparity fell primarily in middle management. Unlike the government, Hoechst directed the salaries to be adjusted. This pay adjustment may have cost the company up front, but it has paid for itself by raising worker productivity.

The government would never direct a pay adjustment unless a rare finding of discrimination had been rendered. Many studies show overwhelming evidence that pay disparities exist within the ranks of white and non-white federal employees. Yet, contrary to the findings of these studies, the government remains oblivious and blatantly ignores the factual evidence presented in the conclusion of these reports. If the results of the study show conclusive evidence of wrong-doing, the government should immediately move to correct the situation.

Addressing the issue of fairness in pay is critical. If the government wants minorities to believe it is serious about treating people fairly, then equitable compensation has to be pursued.

I will never forget the story relayed to me by another employee who was at a meeting presided over by the Commanding General of the installation where I once worked. In the midst of a major reorganization plan, aimed at dealing with the projected manpower cuts, the manager who put the plan together talked about one of the budget positions in logistics being a GS-13. The General interrupted and asked what grade the current environmental budget position was (that was occupied by a black female). The manager sheepishly replied that it was a GS-11.

The General then asked how much money the logistics analyst was responsible for in comparison to the environmental analyst. Needless to say, the environmental analyst had much greater monetary and regulatory responsibility. The manager tried to redeem himself by saying the environmental analyst was being upgraded to a GS-12. Even with the upgrade the environmental analyst would be a full pay grade behind the budget logistician.

Until minorities see tangible evidence of problems being fairly and effectively dealt with, the government will never have their loyalty or trust in matters involving racial fairness. In a global market place, the loyalty and trust of all employees is a force multiplier in terms of quality and productivity.

- **Give top executives experience of what it is**

like to be a minority. At Hoechst Celanese it is mandatory for top executives to join at least two organizations where they are the minority. One senior executive was quoted as saying, "Joining these organizations has been more helpful to me then two weeks of diversity training."

Until decision-makers know what it is like to feel helpless and powerless, it is difficult for them to show sensitivity to the stressful conditions consistently confronted on a daily basis by minorities. Training cannot take the place of real life experience. The government tends to use diversity training as a panacea and then points to it as evidence they are committed to equal employment opportunity.

The government also needs to require Senior Executive Service members to sit on the boards of black universities and actively participate in the education process of our nation's black and other minority students. One of the biggest failures of the Federal government is its lack of effort in recruiting talented minority employees from historically black colleges.

A predominate number of white managers in the Federal government express a reluctance to go to these colleges for recruitment, but do so to honor pre-established mandates and give an appearance of compliance. Talented and educated minorities should be mined like gold; and if treated as such, would provide valuable interchange between the universities and the government in terms of what critical employment needs the government has and what the universities could do to make sure its minority students are educated to meet those needs.

Effective communication between government and academia is essential to breaking down barriers and harmful stereotypes which deter the Federal government from properly managing diversity.

• **Use diversity training.** Again, training should not be viewed as a total solution to the institution of an organization's diversity management or equal opportunity objectives. Managing diversity involves more than scheduling resentful employees to attend classes on racial or gender sensitivity. An effective education program on the importance of diversity requires agencies to include training as a small subset of their overall plan and re-engineered to motivate employees to break out of paradigms regarding racial, cultural and sexual differences.

• **Celebrate differences.** This is the one area the government does fairly well. With Black History Month and various other cultural activities, employees become exposed to positive examples of other cultures. These events must be pursued even more vigorously and employees should be enthusiastically encouraged to participate.

• **Don't lose focus during down-sizing.** Minorities, particularly blacks, are always hit the hardest when an organization begins to down-size. "Last hired, first fired" is an agonizing theme all to familiar to many minorities. When a organization begins to trim its ranks, diversity management becomes all the more important.

The *Fortune* article talked about two companies where blacks were terminated at approximately three times the rate of overall workforce deductions. The article further reported that a black CEO for a packaging company made the remark that, "Many companies have trouble dealing with two major challenges at the same time, managing diversity for the long-term and down- sizing for the short-term." The Federal government has the same problem and all too frequently uses down sizing and hiring freezes as convenient excuses for lack of diversity management.

A number of major companies such as AT&T, Xerox, and Burger King were cited for being able to handle the challenge of down-sizing while simultaneously managing diversity. Xerox CEO, Paul A. Allaire, is quoted as saying that, "Diversity is no fad for us. We remain aggressively affirmative on diversity in tough times as well as good times."

Furthermore, AT&T reportedly monitors reductions by departments and develops creative ways to retain valued employees. Some employees are "loaned" to other departments while others are offered opportunity to take a leave of absence with full benefits. During this time they may elect to further their education with full assurance of re-employment at the same level and pay if a job with the company becomes available.

Burger King also monitors layoffs by department as well as functions. They search a computer run and look for something called the macro pattern. If a person is a poor performer, no matter if they are black, white, Hispanic or Asian, they are let go. However, they make sure no one group suffers disproportionately as compared to the total percent reduction. For example, if the company instituted a 5 percent across the board reduction, management would make sure 12 percent of blacks were not cut. These innovative and practical solutions to monitoring layoffs must be explored by the Federal government.

• **Re-engineer the whole concept of EEO.** The EEOC should be dismantled and an entirely new agency, structured to properly manage diversity, created.

The current EEO program instituted by the Federal government is too dependent on ineffective classroom instruction and weak punitive measures for dealing with infractions. This combination has been woefully inadequate in dealing with the sensitivity surrounding race relations and cultural diversity. It is a system that has white males feeling threatened and minorities feeling powerless. These emotions sap productivity and creates a drag upon the Federal government's efforts to operate at peak efficiency in the face of the emergence of a diverse global community.

Contrary to the rhetoric in the book, *The Bell Curve*, diversity, when managed correctly, adds value to a company's production. In the global market place, no one race of people has all the answers. It takes people of all cultures and life experiences to successfully navigate diverse horizons.

Quotas and preferences can be tossed out if we are now willing to monitor diversity throughout the government to ensure agencies are properly reflecting the talent pool of America. If an agency is 95 percent of any race they are not going to be able to effectively service a culturally diverse global customer base.

The time to act is now! The current mood of the electorate demands change. The question is whether or not we will enact positive change that benefits all Americans or upwardly fan the flames of racial hatred and bigotry. I appeal to Republicans, Democrats, and President Clinton to engage in constructive dialogue which will result in the implementation of a "New Deal" in regards to affirmative action. This would include the interest of all Americans and would verifiably reward those employees who have earned the right to be recognized.

Once lack of racially diverse input is discovered, it is of utmost importance to make the necessary changes to correct these imbalances. It is exponentially more productive to promote or make necessary pay adjustments for qualified minorities than to engage in prolonged litigation of an inherently adversarial nature. No matter who wins, the government loses! We must stop this madness. Our national debt and fiscal survival demands solutions that cut cost and raises productivity. The time is now and the blueprint has just been made available.

CHAPTER 16

A Survival Guide for African-Americans in the Post Democratic Era

African-Americans are at a crossroads. I believe God has allowed us to come to this point to test our faith in Him. Though many of us are pessimistic about the future, I am eternally optimistic because I know who controls the future. I am not concerned about the GOP having control of Congress because God has control of me.

It is time we reassess our failed policies of government dependency and public largess for societal ills such as poverty, black-on-black crime, and illiteracy. We need to take responsibility for our sad state of affairs and lay blame squarely upon our own shoulders.

God never created us to be a race of social lepers. Our race is the progenitor of Kings, Queens, statesmen of the highest order, and heroes that no amount of educational racism could ever bury. The spirit of King Solomon, The Queen of Sheba and other biblical stalwarts cries out to us for affirmative action of the highest sort. Not the kind of affirmative action the government now wants to take away, but the kind which cries out to God to lift us out of the spiritual morass in which we are now entangled.

The Jews found out, as evidenced throughout the Old Testament, that when they obeyed God they prospered, but when they were disobedient, God allowed their enemies to subjugate them. The book of Judges is filled with the sad refrain of entire generations of Jews being held in bondage by idol worshipping heathens, because they did not give the God of Abraham, Issac, and Jacob the proper commitment of faith and obedience.

In the last twenty years, African-Americans have written their own book of Judges. In the fifties and sixties our national resolve spawned the greatest racial revolution this nation has ever seen. At the forefront of our assault on racial bigotry was our faith in the power of God. In answer to our prayers, God sent forth spiritual leaders and through Divine guidance led a race of people out of bondage. These men did for African-Americans what Moses did for the Jews who were under the scathing lash of Pharaoh and the Egyptians.

Sadly, African-Americans have made the same mistake as the Jews when Jews attempted to undue Gods work by collective disobedience to His word and His way. In spite of this tragic and self-imposed curse,

I believe God is willing to offer His grace and chart us on a new course; a course that will make us the head and not the tail.

The theme at the Susquehanna Chapter of Blacks In Government (BIG) luncheon in February 1995 was "Change Is Difficult Yet Necessary." The guest speaker was Elijah Cummings, then Speaker Pro Tem of the Maryland House of Delegates. He told a story of how as a young boy he desired to become a lawyer. When he shared this dream with one of the counselors at his school, the counselor attempted to steal his dream by telling him it was unattainable. Devastated, he went home where his mother encouraged him and continuously nurtured his faith in God.

Upon graduating from law school Cummings was hired by a prestigious law firm. At the end of his first day at work a man showed up desperately seeking the aid of an attorney. As he talked with the man he realized this potential client was the counselor who had attempted to thwart his desire and dream of becoming an attorney. God had made Elijah's enemy his foot stool.

We are now living in a time when African-Americans believe my republican colleagues are trying to steal their dreams. I personally believe they are doing us a huge favor. This fight has never been about politics or white versus black. It has and always will be about good versus evil. By taking away the false God of government give aways, the Republicans are about to unleash the full entrepreneurial genius God has given to our proud and distinguished race. I believe this genius will be unprecedented in the history of America. Here are God's anointed mandates we must follow:

• **Totally Re-dedicate Ourselves as Disciples of Jesus Christ**. Most African-Americans believe the Bible is God's spoken word to mankind and now is our time to repent and re-focus our faith. Once we have completely yielded to God, we can then harness our enormous prayer potential to unleash His power on our behalf. Many may say this is not politically correct to say, but I don't care. "Being politically correct" is relative; God however, is absolute. In order to have His favor, we must repent of our evil ways and yield to His Holy will. When this is done we can be assured of His guidance, and direction.

• **Oust the Politicians Masquerading as Clergy Who Are Nothing More Than Wolves in Sheep's Clothing**. True men of God would never champion a cause against God's will. Yet, we have prominent leaders in the black community who are leading people astray by using civil rights as a cloaking device. Their battle cry is equal rights for all. They promulgate false doctrine and allude that God and sin can coexist. This is damnable hearsay. God will never sanction any cause which goes against his word. The deceptions used by these ministers are the works of Satan. Since he knows the depth of mankind's craving for equality and peace, he uses these causes to destroy us. There are certain groups today who have aligned themselves with civil rights advocates that are an abomination to God. To the shame of African-Americans, our leadership has embraced these groups and by doing so has brought God's disfavor upon us.

Our leadership has also embraced alliances with those who serve false Gods. If an organization declares allegiance to any other than the one true God, then let them be an anathema to us! The great Jewish prophet Elijah asked his nation on Mount Carmel to decide if they were going to serve either Ba'al or the God of their fathers, Abraham, Isaac, and Jacob (1 Kings 18:21). He then challenged the prophets of Ba'al to a showdown in order to prove who was the one true God of the Universe. Even though these false prophets sacrificed animals and prayed from morning to evening, their impotent Gods did nothing (Kings 18:22-29).

Elijah mocked these prophets for serving gods which were utterly powerless to demonstrate their ability before Isreal. After setting up the altar Elijah prayed:

"Hear me, O Lord, hear me, that this people
may know that Thou art the Lord God, and
that Thou hast turned their heart back again."

God then sent fire from heaven to consume the sacrifice and confirm He was indeed God. The Jews fell on their faces and at the direction of Elijah killed the false prophets of Ba'al (1 Kings 18:30-40).

If we want the fire of God to fall on our behalf we must turn away from the modern day prophets of Ba'al. These gods are just as impotent today as they were that eventful day on Mount Carmel. As Elijah asked the Jews, I am now asking African-Americans; Which God are you going to serve? Will we continue to blindly follow these ministerial charlatans or will we turn back to Jesus Christ? As for me and my house, we will serve Christ!

• **Establish a Unified Minority Based Coalition Within the Federal Government.** Since this book is about what's going on in our Federal government, we have to seek out solutions that will effectively address the racial discrimination and have the greatest impact throughout the government at large. When one looks at the identical problems in every agency, it is clear we have been fighting this battle on far too many fronts with very little success. A Minority Coalition is what we need.

At the Department of Agriculture, the minorities have banded together for just such a purpose. Convinced they can accomplish far more together than they would separately, this group of visionaries have actually established a framework which could unite all other minorities in every agency in the government. This type of alliance could ultimately provide hot line telephone numbers for EEO advice and counseling, competent EEO attorneys and sympathetic listeners to people who may not have winnable EEO cases but just need somebody to talk to about their injustices.

We must unify and attack on one primary front. The obvious target is Vice President Gore's National Performance Review and his initiative to Reinvent Government. As one voice we must demand the EEOC be reinvented or dissolved and replaced with a more efficient entity committed to diversification as well as Equal Opportunity. Alliances with the NAACP and Blacks in Government (BIG) may also serve to increase the pool of resources and visibility so desperately needed to sustain such a venture as this.

• **Re-engineer the NAACP.** The presumed demise of the NAACP is one of the sad chapters in African-American history. The largess and strategic miscalculations of the previous leadership is a text book example of how not to operate a nonprofit organization. We must pray that the new leadership does not repeat the mistakes of their predecessors.

Although the election of former congressman, Kweisi Mfume, is a good start, the NAACP must concentrate on insuring that its organization conforms and operates at world-class quality standards. Mr. Mfume should immediately institute a bottoms-up review of every aspect of the organization. Weak and obsolete procedures must be identified and customer focused metrics must be established.

The most efficient charities should be reviewed and their internal processes duplicated if applicable. In order to do this, the NAACP must examine every process that goes on inside these organizations. How do the clerical people at headquarters interact with internal and external customers such as the 2,200 field offices and the general public? The NAACP must institute a policy of high quality customer service.

The March 1995 edition of *Fortune* magazine listed the ten most admired and least admired corporations in America. Corporations that ranked in the most admired status such as Microsoft and Rubbermaid, ranked eight or higher in every category of quality on a scale of one to ten. The ten least admired, such as TWA and K-Mart, were ranked no higher than a four in any quality category. The ten most admired were extremely profitable while the ten least admired were not. The obvious lesson learned was that quality and profitability go hand-in-hand.

Where would the NAACP rank in a category of the most admired or least admired charities in America? Based on what I hear from African-Americans, the consensus can be reasonably determined as undesirable. With approximately 300,000 members and 2,200 field offices, the NAACP has enormous political potential and a bevy of untapped resources. A five year strategic plan with a vision to double its membership and quadruple its donations should be prepared and implemented.

Even with its current membership the NAACP should expect a modest $50 per year contribution from its members. This would give the organization a $15 million financial base to work with every fiscal year. In addition to their membership, a concerted effort should be made to garner every corporate sponsor and charitable foundation dollar they can get.

A full-time staff should be employed to handle this task. Their salaries would be paid by this increase in funding. Additionally, the NAACP should campaign to solicit the backing of all African-American entertainers. There are millions of dollars being paid in taxes by these people that could be donated to the NAACP.

For an organization with as noble a history as the NAACP to be stymied by a $3 million deficit is testimony that its reputation has sunk to an all-time low. Few people believe they are receiving much value for their dollar. African-Americans are no different than any other consumer, wherein, if you can't show them a product is worth having, or in this case supporting, they are not going to part with their hard earned cash.

Even the mechanics of their fund-raising is suspect. As a member, I have never received a solicitation letter from the NAACP asking me to send a donation. This is financial suicide! Although I believe a portion of my membership fee goes to NAACP headquarters, it still doesn't make sense for the organization to not solicit its membership for donations at various times during the year.

Where is the mailing list for its three-hundred-thousand members? A $25 donation per member would have wiped out the deficit and put $4 million in the coffers! My guess is the 2,200 chapters do not work very closely with NAACP headquarters. Again, the reason for this major disconnect can be traced back to a lack of confidence in the vision and direction of the past leadership.

With the election of a new chairwoman, Mrs. Myrile B. Evers-Williams and the confirmation of Mr. Mfume, hopefully this self-defeating direction will change. Given the fact that Mrs. Evers-Williams won the office by only one vote and considering that most of the old guard still remain in key positions of leadership, they both face a daunting task.

• **Abandon Blind Faith Allegiance to the Democratic Party**. African-Americans must stop throwing their political muscle behind Democratic candidates without first understanding the mood of the electorate. Most African-Americans think "conservative" and ironically their values are more closely aligned with Republicans than Democrats. Why then do Blacks overwhelmingly support the Democratic Party in political elections? The answer is simply civil rights. The Democrats are more sympathetic on this issue while the Republicans give it little, if any, attention.

An article in a major magazine quoted Newt Gingrich as saying that, "If the Republicans could ever figure out a way to appeal to African-American voters, they would bury the Democrats." His statement is true. Most African-Americans are for the core issues Republicans tout such as tougher crime laws, lower taxes, family values, balanced budgets, and a strong defense. But their Achilles heel, as the Democrats well know, is civil rights.

The Republicans assault on affirmative action and their targeting of welfare recipients as scapegoats while allowing corporate welfare to go unchecked to the tune of $55 billion a year does not endear them to the black vote. In spite of the Republicans unwillingness thus far to adequately address the concerns of African-Americans in relation to civil rights, the black organizations must not thoughtlessly endorse Democratic candidates.

Although the Republican party as a whole has been unsympathetic on this issue, there are candidates who have shown a willingness to listen to the concerns of the African-American community. The NAACP should begin to do its homework on all potential Republican candidates and then decide to endorse the candidate who best exemplifies Christian values and has an understanding of the need to insure minorities are included in mainstream economics of America.

This understanding must be accompanied by a resolve to initiate and protect policies which help qualified minorities compete in our society. We can no longer be a one party race; groups such as the NAACP can be instrumental in making this happen.

• **Plan for an America Without Affirmative Action**. It is obvious that affirmative action is going to be overturned or greatly modified. The Republican majority in

Congress has decided the American people want a change. The process of whittling away at affirmative action began during the Reagan years. By staffing the courts with anti-affirmative action judges, legal precedents were already being set before this current Congress was even in power. The NAACP and African-Americans can continue to bark at the moon or accept the dawning of a new day. If we are wise and realize the inevitable, we can focus our talents on effective alternatives.

Opponents of affirmative action argue that no group should be given preference over another. Most Americans (black or white) totally agree with this noble proclamation. African-Americans just don't believe these words will be backed up by deeds. Our fears are accurate.

White America has been deluded into believing minorities no longer need programs which insure fair representation. CEO's like Ernest Drew of Hoechst Celanese are few and far between. Given this fact and the current political climate in Washington, the NAACP needs to be proactive in formulating a post affirmative action agenda.

In the February 27, 1995, edition of *Business Week* an article entitled "A Race-Neutral Helping Hand," some possible adaptations to affirmative action were discussed. These ideas can serve as the starting point for positive dialogue between affirmative action advocates and its opponents.

• **Limit Breaks To Needy**. Many opponents believe well-off minorities reap the benefits of affirmative action and they resent it. If some type of eligibility requirements could be established, this might assuage the resentment of opponents.

• **Restrict Use By New Immigrants**. California has shown that anti-immigration sentiment is building throughout the country. Although this sentiment is unhealthy and could lead to hatred and bigotry, this country cannot continue to support the worlds outcast. Some types of restrictions on affirmative action are inevitable.

• **Foster Diversity**. I introduced this idea in the previous chapter and the NAACP would be wise to champion it through Congress. Affirmative action has a negative connotation and we must get away from its stigma. Benchmarking private industries methodology for fostering diversity is not only wise but an imperative.

• **Black Self-Help**. The NAACP should form partnerships with other organizations to assist qualified blacks in obtaining educational and employment opportunities. Networking with corporate America and institutions of higher learning is essential. Combining our collective economic and intellectual resources will make us a far more formidable opponent than various factions going it alone.

The April 1995 issue of *Black Enterprise* carried a quote from Oscar J. Coffey, president of the U.S. African-American Chamber of Commerce. He stated that, "Black churches take millions of dollars to white-owned banks every Monday morning. We can be far, far more effective in dealing with city hall, with business interests and certainly with leading institutions if we organize our banking and purchasing efforts wherever we live, so that we can have an impact and influence on the people we do business with . . . We have within ourselves important seeds of our own economic development . . . Certainly, we must do more joint venturing with other groups."

The same edition of *Black Enterprise* contained an article on an organization called The Joint Center for Political and Economic Studies. This African-American think-tank has been around for 25 years, and done yeomen's work in helping to shape the economic and political agendas which could benefit black America. This type of intellectual resource must be used to the greatest extent possible.

According to the article, the group is currently working on a study to research the employment potential of minority-owned businesses. They are also looking at the types of training employees receive in minority firms as well as their opportunities for upward mobility. They are trying to determine if there is a strategy that exist in minority businesses (in regards to supporting members of the minority workforce) which could be deployed in other businesses and communities.

The fact that the Center is non-partisan gives its data credibility when being used to identify the impact of legislation coming out of Washington on the black community. This information is essential to combat the rising tide of anti-affirmative action and set-aside sentiment which the country is now experiencing.

These are but a few areas of discussion which could lead to valuable alternatives to affirmative action. The bottom line is blacks and other minorities want assurance that opportunities will not be closed. Segments of white America want preferences based solely on race to stop. I believe both of these objectives can be obtained if we are willing to collectively re-engineer the process.

• **Openly Challenge Vocal Opponents of Affirmative Action**. In a very real sense African-Americans are facing a challenge as sinister as Jim Crow and other racist policies that attempted to segregate them from the mainstream of society. Republicans are in effect saying "blacks and other minorities are doing fine; let's freeze everything in place and get rid of all vehicles that helped minorities realize what little progress they received." Our response to this assault upon our civil rights should be nonviolent intellectual protest that engages our opponents in substantive debate.

The reason the Republican's *Contract With America* is so appealing to white people of this country is because so much was wrong with the policies of the past. If we are not willing to admit that much of their agenda is best for America, then we are just as hypocritical as they are on their misguided stand against affirmative action. We must be their biggest cheer leaders on deficit reduction, legal reforms, school prayers, and term limits.

On the issue of affirmative action we must state the facts. Our message to them should be: "If you want to pit white America against black America, we will expose you by joining forces with all minorities who stand to lose as much if not more then we do." One must remember that the biggest recipients of affirmative action are white females. As a minority they will surely be troubled by the Republicans' anti-affirmative action policies

We must no longer be frightened by the candidness of Rush Limbaugh and Newt Gingrich. Again, on some issues they are right. When it comes to affirmative action they are wrong! Remember the truth always outlasts a lie. The truth is that affirmative action is not causing wide spread reverse-discrimination and an inferior workforce that can't compete globally. In fact the reverse is true.

Glass ceilings and other quasi-barriers have robbed America of a sorely needed talent pool bulging with new ideas of entrepreneurial genius. These ideas would create new jobs by identifying new markets, and would spike our productivity and global competitiveness. Armed with this information we should go forth and be prepared to challenge the opponents of workforce

diversity to a national debate at any place and anytime.
• **Change the Focus of Black History Month**. Too much
of Black History Month focuses on the past. Certainly
the noble exploits of our predecessors and their collective legacy must be taught and retained. Even sordid
aspects of the past such as slavery need to be exposed
to this and future generations.

However, kids today need positive role models that
are current and relevant. All to often thousands of
black students dread when February comes around and
are relieved when its over. Is this what the framers of
Black History Month had in mind? I don't think so.
Much of Black History Month should focus on successful blacks in the business and entertainment world.

I would stress more business than entertainment
to counter racist stereotypes that blacks are only good
at athletics and other forms of leisure activity. The
April 1995 issue of *Black Enterprise* carried the picture
of Ben & Jerry's CEO Robert Holland who heads the
very successful ice cream company. Both Ben and Jerry
are white yet they chose Mr. Holland, a black man,
because of his impeccable credentials and proven track
record of success.

The same article talked about other successful black
men and women in the financial management field who
collectively manage billions in assets for a diverse cli-
entele. These are the people our children need to see
and their stories need to be told. When this happens
our country will began to see a gleam in the eyes of the

black youth. This gleam will give birth to positive aspirations and maybe one day entire generations of black males will no longer be incarcerated or killed by drug or gang related violence. This dream is obtainable if we just make a new start.

• **Take Control of Our Inner Cities**. It is no secret that Satan has gotten control of inner cities and waged war on blacks, particularly our males. We must devise a solution to retake these cities from our adversary. Our first step, as always, is to petition God for deliverance!

What has government dependence done for the situation? I have always believed the Federal government could stop the massive flow of drugs into America's cities if it desired. It is my contention that blacks are viewed as cannon fodder and Congress really does not care about the demise of our urban centers. This lethargy is short-sighted and will ultimately contribute to the downfall of our country.

In each city I believe there are programs already in place which are helping to lift thousands of underprivileged citizens out of poverty and hopelessness. These programs are sponsored by local governments, churches, and other volunteer associations. The best of these initiatives should be bench-marked and a massive networking effort should be undertaken. This effort could be spearheaded by the NAACP in conjunction with other organizations.

Government tax dollars should not be counted on as the financial foundation for this effort. There are millions of dollars in private contributions which would flow into such an undertaking if we all become committed. We can and must develop a vision for our survival that is not predicated on the budgets in Washington. What is possible for us to do we must do by faith! What appears to be impossible to do we must also do by faith!

Will the NAACP make the changes necessary to gain God's favor and re-emerge as the organization spiritually endowed to lead African-Americans out of the spiritual and economic morass we are in? Time will only tell. If it decides to remain stoic and uncompromising in regards to the failed policies of the past, God will accelerate its decline to the ash heap of historical oblivion. The spiritual re-awakening of African-Americans will happen with or without the NAACP. It is my fervent prayer it will decide to do the right thing!

CHAPTER 17

What to Do
When Faced with
On-the-Job Discrimination

Many employees who work for the Federal government and even those of you who are employed in the private sector, will have questions about what you should do and where you should go when confronted with a discriminatory situation in the workplace. The following avenues will serve as a guide to steer you through this process:

• **Contact an EEO Counselor:** In the Federal government, the EEO Counselor is the first step in a long and tedious complaint processing journey. As in any occupation some EEO Counselors are very good and some are not so good. Before you contact a counselor, check around and see if other employees will recommend somebody. This is where it pays to be a member of a minority organization such as Blacks In Government. BIG members will almost always have valuable information to share with other employees in need.

When you file an EEO complaint be prepared for a long journey. Most complaints take years to process, especially when appeals are involved. Some EEO Counselors will try to resolve your complaint during the informal process by getting both you and management to compromise. For this reason, make sure you know exactly what you are willing to compromise on.

• **Hire a Competent Attorney Proficient in EEO Litigation:** If you are prepared to do whatever is necessary to win your EEO case, find a good attorney. If you can find one who will charge you a reasonable retainer and take a percentage of the award, hire him as early in the process as possible. Competent legal representation dramatically increases your chances of getting a favorable agreement with your agency. Do not depend on receiving free legal aid from the NAACP or some other civil rights organization. This kind of assistance is more the exception then the rule. By all means check into it, but don't rely on getting it.

• **Research Your Rights Under the Merit Systems Protection Board (MSPB):** In addition to filing a EEO complaint some actions such as removals, suspensions for more than 14 days, demotions, separations, denials of within-grade increases and forced retirements may be appealed to MSPB. These are called mixed cases. In some instances you will have remedies under MSPB that are more favorable and timely than under the EEO system. In addition, if your appeal to MSPB is dismissed for jurisdictional reasons you still maintain your right to contact an EEO counselor and file a EEO complaint. In essence you get two shots at the target.

Another plus for MSPB is the possibility that a supervisor could be reprimanded if the alleged injustice is upheld. This certainly does not apply in all cases but it is possible. Under EEO, the chances are extremely remote that a supervisor would be reprimanded even if you prevail in your complaint. Many complainants file EEO cases thinking the supervisor can receive an adverse action based upon their complaint. This is not available under the EEO process.

MSPB can be an attractive option for an employee under certain situations. Whatever you do, research your rights and consult with a competent government official.

• **Consider an Alternative Dispute Resolution Program:** Alternative Dispute Resolution involves the complainant and management agreeing to allow a third party to mediate their conflict. If management and the employee can come to an agreement, you have a win-win situation instead of the current lose-lose environment inherent in the EEO process. It's win-win because both parties walk away feeling productive instead of disgruntled and bitter.

This is probably going to be the vehicle of choice in the not-too-distant future. More and more agencies are looking into programs that specialize in dispute resolution. The organizations that are using them are finding the process timely and extremely cost effective. Check with your local EEO Officer and see if a program exist where you work. If it does not, actively campaign for one to get started. Remember someone has to get the ball rolling.

• **Contact a Union Representative:** If you are a member of a union, don't hesitate to get them involved. I am by no means an expert in this area, but I do know that these representatives can be an important ally when you are in a confrontation with management.

• **Call Your Congressional Representative:** People do not make good use of their elected officials. In this information age, many of your elected officials can be contacted by electronic mail or fax. They will make an inquiry on your behalf if you request it. Get to know where their local offices are located and stop by to make yourself known. This may be beneficial to you at a later time.

• **Join a Minority Interest Group Organization:** Many African-Americans miss the boat on this one. Whether it be the halls of Congress or the installations and agencies we work for, interest groups are listened to. The old adage that there is strength in numbers applies here. These organizations such as the local chapter of the NAACP or Blacks in Government (BIG) can prove to be invaluable when you are faced with an adverse employment situation. Leveraging our collective intellect and resources is a mandatory prerequisite for dealing with the challenges in this post democratic era.

• **Private Sector:** For those who do not work for the government you can file EEO complaints directly with the Equal Employment Opportunity Commission (EEOC). Unlike the public sector, private enterprises will probably not have in-house EEO counselors for you to consult with. This makes it more imperative to hire competent legal counsel. Also check with your Human Resources Department and see what avenues are available for conflict resolution.

Here are some agencies that may be willing to assist you if you have an EEO complaint (Keep in mind the following addresses and phone numbers may have changed, but getting the current information should be easy):

• **Your Local Chapter of the NAACP:** Some chapters are more proactive then others. Talk to a representative and find out what you have to do to get them involved. It helps if you are a dues paying member. The cost to join is minimal and the benefit of having them as an ally is well worth the expense.

• **The NAACP Legal Defense Fund, INC. (LDF):** Many people are under the impression that the LDF works for the NAACP. This is not true. They are for the most part totally separate organizations. They may be willing to provide you legal assistance. Since resources are a problem they are very selective as to what cases they will take. It may be a long shot but it is certainly worth a phone call or a letter. Their number is (212) 219-1900 or Fax (212) 226-7592. The mailing address is NAACP

Legal Defense And Educational Fund, Inc., Suite 1600, 99 Hudson Street, NY, NY 10013-2897. This is the national office and they may have local affiliates.

• **The Lawyer's Committee for Civil Rights Under Law:** This is another organization that could possibly provide legal aid. They too are selective as to what cases they will pursue. Their number is (202) 662-8600 or fax (202) 783-0857. Mailing address is 1450 G. Street, N.W., Suite 400, Washington, DC 20005.

• **The Washington Lawyer's Committee for Urban Affairs:** This organization is affiliated with the above agency but they will consider offering their assistance once they review the merits of your case. Their number is (202) 835-0031 or fax (202) 835-0309.

• **The Local Chapter of the American Civil Liberties Union (ACLU):** You can find their phone number in your telephone directory. They may refer you to another source but again, its worth a call.

• **Call Your Congressional Representative:** There is a site on the internet called Club Fed which has a listing of Congressional phone numbers, fax numbers, and e-mail addresses. The internet address for Club Fed is http://www.clubfed.com/. Two other internet addresses for Congressional representatives are ftp:// shemesh.spa.umn.edu/juan/contactingcongress.txt and gopher://una.hh.lib.umich.edu:70/00/socsci/poliscilaw/ uslegi/conemail.

• **Get Your Local Church Involved:** Don't underestimate this resource. If you are actively involved in the church and support it financially, your pastor will have a vested interest in helping you with an EEO situation at your place of employment, particularly if it involves a termination. A well-written letter signed by your minister can serve notice to your employer that you intend to fight this injustice with every resource you have. The key is visibility. Most employers despise negative publicity and are willing to compromise to avoid it. If your church is large enough there may even be attorneys who are willing to assist church members at a reduced cost.

• **Above All Else, Pray:** My avenues of approach are determined by my guidance from Jesus Christ through the moving of His Holy spirit. All the above information I have given you should be predicated on what Christ wants you to do!

Where Do We Go From Here?

B ased on my employment experiences as a minority working for the Department of Defense, my personal investigations as an EEO Counselor, and the horrific accounts from so many agencies depicted in this book, it is obvious that rampant employment discrimination exists within the Federal government. I know many minorities in the system who are suffering from what I call "employee alienation." This happens when management treats some employees as if they are small school children who only need to be tolerated, but never taken seriously.

African-American employees overwhelmingly receive the brunt of this cold shoulder approach from supervisors and co-workers. This tactic has a devastating psychological effect on many bright, energetic, and enthusiastic black employees who would love to unleash their intrapreneurial genius on the myriad of problems facing Uncle Sam everyday. Sadly, this genius is either trampled upon or stolen and the credit is attributed to someone else. The result of this wanton injustice is an inferior product for the taxpayer and an unproductive and disgruntled employee for the Federal government.

The anti-affirmative action bunch are the culprits which have shaped the attitudes of white America and created a swarm of resentments which flies in the face of minority employees everyday. While this group has repeatedly lambasted affirmative action in the media, they have yet to speak about any alternatives which will insure America is not cheated out of a vast talent pool of minority employees.

One of the biggest slaps in the face for black Americans was when Congress decided to pay the families of Japanese citizens who were interned during World War II. To make these payments without any regard for the millions of slaves who were illegally and immorally held in bondage was the ultimate affront to black America. It is as if this country believes the debt to black America has been paid in full.

The classic example of how God deals with a nation that illegally benefits from slave labor is found in the book of Exodus. When Pharaoh finally relented and decided to let the Jews go free, God made the Egyptians give the Jews a huge percentage of their wealth as payment for 400 years of bondage (Exodus 12:30-36).

Although America will never make good on this debt, it can certainly continue, albeit slowly thus far, to commit to initiatives which promote equality and economic prosperity for all its citizens. To pursue policies which isolate minorities, particularly blacks, the affirmative action forces will splinter this country into warring factions based upon race and economic class. This will erode America from within and make it vulnerable from without.

As African-Americans, we must all come together under one banner of righteousness. Political affiliations aside, we must doggedly pursue an agenda that is not only morally right for us, but for the rest of America as well. We can never be satisfied as long as the black male is being eradicated, and our children are being "held hostage" in our inner cities.

Also, before we shift the burdens prevalent in our culture to the Federal government, we must mobilize every possible resource at the grass roots level. Until we take care of our own we can expect no sentiment from the rest of America.

Jesus yesterday, Jesus today and Jesus forever! With Him lies victory. Without Him defeat and ruin await. The path God wants us to take is laid out before us. Satan can neither hide it nor stop our advance. However, the choice to take it resides with us. As I said in the beginning, this book is not being written in anger, but with a quiet assurance its time has come.

Selected Bibliography

Bowman, Tom. "NSA Has Poor Record On Hiring," *The Baltimore Sun*, August 17, 1993.

Bridger, Chet. "Largest Hispanic Lawsuit Goes to Trial," *Federal Times*.

---"Minorities Held Back at Base, Report Says," *Federal Times*.

Carter, Stephen. *Reflections of an Affirmative Action Baby*. New York: Harper Collins, 1991.

City of Richmond vs. J.A. Croson Company, 488 U.S. 469 (1989)

Cose, Ellis. *The Rage of a Privileged Class*. New York: Harper Collins, 1993.

Federal Employees News Digest, September 19, 1994

Fletcher, Michael A. "In Md. Delegation Only Bentley Has No Black or Hispanic Aides," *The Baltimore Sun*.

---"Mikulski Introduces Fair Employment Legislation for the Capitol's 2300 Workers," *The Baltimore Sun*, June 16, 1994.

Fourteenth Amendment - Equal Protection Clause, U.S. Constitution.

Harris, Christy. "Black Navy Workers Harassment," *Federal Times*, August 16, 1993.

---"Discrimination Allegations Center for Disease Control," *Federal Times*.

Herrnstein, Richard J. and Murray, Charles J. *The Bell Curve*. New York: The Free Press, 1994.

"How Do Market Leaders Keep Their Edge," *Fortune Magazine*, February 6, 1995.

Hughes, Ken. "Equal Employment Opportunity Commission," *Federal Times*, August 8, 1993.

"Judges Forbid Scholarships Based on Race," *The Baltimore Sun*, October 28, 1994.

Larson, Richard. *Sue Your Boss Rights and Remedies for Employment Discrimination*. Giroux: 1981.

Meddis, Sam V. "No Retreat Expected in Judicial Appointments," *USA Today*, November 18-20, 1994.

Morganthau, Tom. "IQ Is It Destiny," *Newsweek*, October 24, 1994.

Podberesky, Daniel J. vs. University of Maryland.

Rice, Faye. "How To Make Diversity Pay," *Fortune Magazine*, May 8, 1994.

Rivenbark, Leigh. "Black Workers Bash Commerce for Bias," *Federal Times*, June 13, 1994.

---"FBI Agents Oppose Bias Settlement," *Federal Times*, May 24, 1993.

---"Race Bias Lawsuit Could Be Biggest Ever," *Federal Times*, March 14, 1994.

Thompson Chain Reference Bible, King James Version, B.B., Kirkbride Co., Inc. 1982.

Title II Civil Rights Act of 1991, Sector 202

University of California vs. Bakke, 488 U.S. 265 (1978).

Walker, Meg. "Battling Race Discrimination at Agriculture," *Federal Times*, October 31, 1994.

Wards Cove Packing vs. Atonio 490 U.S. 642 (1989).

Index

A

Affirmative action, 73, 100
  definition of, 15
  Federal government practices,
    13–14
  impact of Nixon admin., 12
  laws of, 15
  myths of, 13
  policy of, 15
  quotas, 13, 16
  reasons for opposition,
    16, 19
  Republicans assault on, 12
  use by the media, 15
  white females as beneficiaries
    of, 51
  Republicans who support, 12
Allaire, Paul A., 107
Alternative Dispute Resolution,
  132
American Civil Liberties Union,
  135
American Council on Education,
  33
Anti-affirmative action groups,
  13
Apple Computer, 90
Asian-American employees
  discrimination against within
    USDA, 71
Asian-Americans, 70
AT&T, 90, 107
Atwell, Robert H., 33

B

Bakke, Alan, 22
Baltimore Sun, 37, 38
Bell Curve, The, 84, 85–
  95, 98, 99, 108
  premise of, 87
Ben & Jerry's, 127
Benjamin Banneker Scholarship,
  32, 35
Bentley, Helen, 38
Black Enterprise, 123, 124, 127
Black interns
  treatment of, 55
Black managers
  recruitment of, 53
  treatment of other blacks, 73
Blacks in Government (BIG),
  41, 113, 117, 133
Blacks in technical positions
  treatment of, 54
Border Patrol Agents, 62
  black agents employed as, 62
  number of blacks in INS, 63
Bridger, Chet, 46, 49
Brown, Ron, 76
Burger King, 107, 108
Business Week, 122

C

Carter, Stephen L., 18
Casellas, Gilbert, 82
Center for Disease Control
  discrimination practices, 65–
    68
*City of Richmond v. J.A. Croson
  Company,* 27, 28

dissenting opinion by
Thurgood Marshall, 28
Supreme Court decision, 27
Civil Rights Act of 1964, 22
Civil Rights Act of 1991, 24
Coalition of Minority
Employees, 70
Coffey, Oscar J., 123
Cognitive elite, 89
major blunders of, 90–91
Commerce Committee for
African-American Con-
cerns, 75
Committee for African-Ameri-
can Concerns, 76
confronting discrimination
within Commerce Depart-
ment, 76
*Conflict of Rights, The Supreme
Court and Affirmative
Action, 17*
Congressional Representation
in cases of job discrimination,
133
Contract With America, 125
Cose, Elliot, 25
Cummings, Elijah, 113

D

*Daniel J. Podberesky v. Univer-
sity of Maryland,* 32
Department of Agriculture
discrimination practices, 69–
74
Department of Commerce
discrimination practices, 76–
78

Department of Defense
discrimination within, 23–26
Department of Health and
Human Services, 65
Department of the Navy
discrimination within, 45
Discrimination
in Federal government, 19
Discriminatory complaints
how complaints are handled
by government, 67
Diversity, 98, 108
adding value, 108
managing and implementing,
98–99
Diversity training, 106
Dorn, Edwin, 23
Drew, Earnest H., 97, 100

E

EEO complaint process, 76
EEO Counselor
use of in cases of job discrimination, 130
EEO litigation
hiring a competent attorney,
131
Eglin Air Force Base
discrimination within base, 46
Employees with disabilities, 70
Employment discrimination
at Capitol of USA, 37
Equal Employment Opportunity
Commission (EEOC), 68,
78, 108, 134
record of handling complaints,
80–84

re-engineering the concept, 108

Espy, Mike, 71, 72, 73, 74

Evers-Williams, Myrile B., 120

F

FBI
  number of black agents, 58

FBI Agents Association, 57, 59, 60

Federal Bureau of Investigation
  discrimination practices, 57–61

Federal Employees News Digest, 23, 82

Federal Plantation, 14

Federal Times, 45, 46, 49, 57, 62, 65, 69, 75, 80

Fletcher, Arthur
  and affirmation action, 12

Fletcher, Michael A., 37, 38

Fortune, 90, 91, 97, 98, 100, 107

G

Gates, Bill, 90

General Accounting Office
  (GAO) study of Capitol
  workers, 37, 80

Gingrich, Newt, 120, 126

"Glass ceiling, 16, 24, 25, 70, 74, 126

"Good old boy network," 41

H

Harris, Christy, 45, 65

Herrnstein, Richard J., 86, 87

Hispanics, 70
  discrimination of in Air Force, 49

Hoechst Celanese, 97, 100, 103, 105
  work-force diversity practices, 97–99

Holland, Robert, 127

How to Sue Your Boss, 29

Hughes, Ken, 80

I

IBM, 90

Immigration and Naturalization
  Service, 62
  discrimination practices, 62–64

J

Japanese citizens, restitution of, 138

Job Discrimination
  steps to takes, 130–136

Joint Center for Political and
  Economic Studies, 124

K

Keller, George, 33

Kelly Air Force Base, 50
  discrimination within, 49

Kemp, Jack, 89

L

Larson, Richard, E., 29

"last plantation" (referring to
  USDA), 69

Lawyer's Committee for Civil Rights Under Law, 135
Limbaugh, Rush, 126
Lucas, Lawrence, 71

M

Managing diversity, 98
McCaw Cellular, 91
Merit Systems Protection Board, 131
Mfume, Kweisi, 117
Microsoft, 90
Mikulski, Barbara, 38
Military installations discrimination within, 40
Minority Coalition, 116
Morganthau, Tom, 87
Munoz, Manuel, 50
Murray, Charles, 86, 87
Myers, Marcia, 32

N

NAACP, 46, 76, 117, 133
NAACP Legal Defense Fund, 134
National Performance Review, 117
National Security Agency, 52
employment discrimination, 52–56
Newsweek, 87

O

Office of Civil Rights Enforcement, 70

P

Podberesky, Daniel J., 32
Powell, Colin, 12
Protected class white males as, 17

Q

Quotas, 16, 18, 73
in regards to affirmative action, 13

R

Racial quotas, 17–18
Rage Of A Privileged Class, The 25
Reagan administration Supreme Court judges, 34
Reagan/Bush administrations, 27–31
impact on affirmative action programs, 27
Reflections Of An Affirmative Action Baby, 18
Republicans assault on affirmative, 121
Reverse discrimination, 13, 26, 60
racially biased application, 21
myth of, 21–22
Rice, Faye, 97
Rivenbark, Leigh, 57, 62, 75
Ross, David, 63

S

Scholarship programs as impacted by Reagan/Bush Administrations, 33

Simon, Senator Paul, 82
Smith, Grover, 101
Smith, Michael A., 53
Southern Christian Leadership
    Council, 48
Special agents, in INS
    percentage of blacks employes
      as, 63
Supreme Court judges, 34
    racial mix under Clinton
      administration, 35

T

Thomas, Clarence, 73, 82

U

U.S. African-American Chamber
    of Commerce, 123
Union Representation
    in cases of job discrimination,
    133
University of California v.
    Bakke, 22
Urofsky, Melvin I., 17
USA Today, 34
USDA
    Minority Coalitions recom-
    mendations for improve-
    ments, 71–72

W

Walker, Meg, 69
Wards Cove Packing v. Atonio,
    30
Washington Lawyer's Commit-
    tee for Urban Affairs, 135

Washington Lawyers Committee
    on Civil Rights, 81
White females as beneficiaries of
    affirmative action, 51
White males
    and affirmative action, 18
White managers
    discrimination against blacks
      psychology of, 86–87
    reluctance to hire blacks, 55–
      56
Women's groups, 70
Work-force diversity, 53

X

Xerox, 107